Living Authentically:
8 Steps to
Transformation

Andrea L. Dudley

Living Authentically: 8 Steps to Transformation
By Andrea L. Dudley

© 2015 Andrea L. Dudley
Printed in the United States of America
ISBN 978-0-692-62872-0

All rights reserved sole by the author. The author guarantees all contents are original and do not infringe upon the legal rights of any other person or work. No part of this book may be reproduced, stored in a retrieval system, or transmitted in any form or by any means without expressed written permission of the author.

All quotes, unless otherwise noted, are from the New King James Version. Copyright 1979, 1980, 1982 by Thomas Nelson, Inc. Used by permission. All rights reserved.

Scriptures marked KJV are taken from The Holy Bible, King James Version. Copyright © 1972 by Thomas Nelson Inc., Camden, New Jersey 08103.

Scriptures marked AMP are taken from The Amplified Bible, containing the amplified Old Testament and the amplified New Testament. 1987. The Lockman Foundation: La Habra, CA

Scriptures marked MSG are taken from The Message Bible. Published by permission. Originally published by NavPress in English as THE MESSAGE: The Bible in Contemporary Language copyright 2002 by Eugene Peterson. All rights reserved. (*The Message Bible Online*)

Scriptures marked ISV are taken from the International Standard Version **(ISV)** Copyright © 1995-2014 by ISV Foundation. All Rights Reserved Internationally. Used by permission of Davidson Press, LLC.

Scriptures marked NIV are taken from the HOLY BIBLE, NEW INTERNATIONAL VERSION. Copyright © 1973, 1978, 1984 by International Bible Society. Used by permission of Zondervan Publishing House. All rights reserved.

Editors: Dr. Larry Keefauver, Pam McLaughlin
Cover Design: Habakkuk Publishing

Printed in the U.S.A.

Dedication

This book is dedicated to those who recognize the need for change in their lives and are willing to put in the work to make it happen. Our hope is that, as a result of reading this book, you will take courage and change your life for the better.

It is also dedicated to the tribe of people who love and support me on a daily basis in real life, through Facebook and other social media outlets. I love and appreciate each of you.

To my loving and amazing husband, Michael, and my three gifted children, Solomon, Princeton and Andrea Amere. To my granddaughter, Ashlyn Hope. To my sister, Sima Ballinger. You are all my family, I love you dearly! I've learned so much from you all about life and love and what matters most.

I am so excited about the big dreams that you have. Never allow anyone to steal your dreams. Harness the power of dreams by giving yourself permission to dream with God and to tap into who God created you to be. Thank you for giving me the gift of having you in my life!

Anthologies published by Habakkuk Publishing

TALITHA CUMI:
MOTHERS OF THE NATIONS ARISE!

TALITHA CUMI:
DAMSEL I SAY UNTO THEE ARISE!

TALITHA CUMI:
DAUGHTERS ARISE!

TALITHA CUMI:
MOTHERS & DAUGHTERS ARISE

TALITHA CUMI:
GET UP GIRL

TALITHA CUMI:
IT'S POSSIBLE
LIVING BEYOND LIMITATIONS

TALITHA CUMI:
DREAM AGAIN
AWAKING THE DREAMER INSIDE OF YOU

Table of Contents

Dedication	iii
Chapter 1 You Don't Know What You Don't Know	1
Chapter 2 Unleashing the Power Within	13
Chapter 3 Unlimited Resources	23
Chapter 4 Make a Decision	31
Chapter 5 Discovering Your Authentic Self	37
Chapter 6 Rule Your World	47
Chapter 7 Overcoming Obstacles	61
Chapter 8 Alignment	71
Chapter 9 The Bucket List	91
Chapter 10 I Am a Witness	103
Chapter 11 The Eight-Step Transformation Process Part 1	113
Chapter 12 The Eight-Step Transformation Process Part 2	131
Chapter 13 Regaining My Confidence after a Setback	151
Chapter 14 Maintaining Your Authenticity	169
Conclusion	181
Acknowledgements	185
About the Author	188

CHAPTER 1
You Don't Know What You Don't Know

You do not know how powerful you are until you need to tap into the power that resides inside of you. It is an inside job. Yes, the power resides inside of you.

Immaculée Ilibagiza's idyllic world was ripped apart in 1994, when Rwanda descended into a bloody genocide that ultimately claimed the lives of more than a million people. Immaculée found herself immediately going from a college student with "a beautiful life" to an individual who did whatever she had to do to survive. For ninety-one days, she and seven other women hid in the cramped bathroom of a local pastor's home while hundreds of machete-wielding killers hunted for them. She lived to tell her story, and was able to pull from within the courage needed to survive. Chances are she had no idea the strength that resided within her.

We all possess a strength or a supernatural power within us, waiting for us to call on it bringing it to the forefront.

I had an opportunity to participate in an online seminar where Immaculée was the guest speaker. She shared with great emotion, clarity, and thought how this transformational moment in life led her to destiny's path. Her amazing story was both encouraging and inspiring. It is a testament of the strength that lies within the human spirit and our ability to go passed our comfort zone when confronted with life threatening or challenging obstacles. She was able to tap into her inner spirit which supplied her with the wherewithal to endure a tremendous hardship.

We all possess this strength or a supernatural power within waiting for us to call on it to bring it to the forefront. God has allotted to each of us a measure of faith. Stories of ordinary human beings performing extraordinary acts are in no way uncommon. We have all heard them like the father running into his burning house to save his child that comes out unscathed with his child. The husband and wife lost in the mountains who survived for seven days without food or water. Peter, who walked on water! Moses, who led the Israelites out of Egypt across the Red Sea on dry land, and the list goes on. These extraordinary acts of faith and strength come from our inner man. They are from a power, if never given the need to tap into, would never be realized.

Superman

As a child I used to love watching the movie Superman. The introduction of the show went something like this:

"Faster than a speeding bullet! More powerful than a locomotive! Able to leap tall buildings at a single bound!"

"Look up in the sky! It's a bird! It's a plane! It's Superman!"

"Yes, it's Superman, strange visitor from another planet who came to Earth with powers and abilities far beyond those of mortal men. Superman, who can change the course of mighty rivers, and bend steel in his bare hands. Who, disguised as Clark Kent, mild-mannered reporter for a great metropolitan newspaper, fights a never ending battle for truth, justice, and the American way."

I was fascinated with the exploits of this superman. I guess inside of each of us there is a yearning to do something great or to help someone. Fast forward to Man of Steel, a 2013 American superhero film based on the DC Comics character Superman. The film is a reboot of the *Superman* film series that portrays the character's origin story. In it, a young boy (Clark) learns that he has extraordinary powers and is not of this Earth. As a young man, he journeys to discover where he came from and what he was sent here to do. Eventually the hero in him must emerge if he is to save the world from annihilation and become the symbol of hope for all mankind.

In one of the scenes Clark is riding on a bus to school. The bus driver loses control and the bus careens into a lake. With little hesitation Clark dives out of the back of the bus into the water and delivers the bus to dry ground with all passengers safely in tow. Now you are thinking what does this have to do with anything?

Inside each of us is a superhero just waiting for the *karios* moment in time to release that inner power and do what we were created to do. Although we did not come from planet Krypton in a spacecraft, we all possess the power to do exploits beyond our natural ability. We all have the capacity to do something extraordinary which will impact the world.

My assignment is to help you realize your true potential and for you to start living above and beyond your highest expectations. I will show you how to break passed the place you are in and move into what you may have always thought was impossible.

It Is Possible

In this day and age more than ever before, people are discovering that inside of them is a power which is endless, strength that is resilient, billows of peace waiting to consume them, victory wanting to encapsulate defeat, and possibilities waiting to be called upon. People are searching for love, happiness, peace, tranquility, and they want to know why they were created.

Buddhist, Catholic, Atheist, Christian, and non-Christian are all asking the same questions. What is my purpose? Why was I created? Thought leaders Anthony Robbins, Zig Ziglar, Oprah, Dr. Oz, Bishop T. D. Jakes, Deepak Chopra, Iyanla Vanzant, and Joel Osteen are encouraging us to tap into this unseen potential. On every continent of the world people want to know how to go to the next level. How do we break through or break out? How can we be more, get more, and do more? There is an innate nagging on the inside of us that keeps prompting us, "You can do better. There is more. Keep striving. Do not settle."

I am no different—I do want more. I want to help more people to have more. I want to help more people to become who they were created to be. I am on a journey of discovery. I am striving to be all that my creator created me to be so that I can help others with their own self-discovery.

People everywhere are discovering that inside of them is a power which is endless, strength that is resilient, billows of peace waiting to consume them, victory wanting to encapsulate defeat, and possibilities waiting to be called upon.

Inside each of us is the potential to do something great. Philosophers, scientists, and theologians believe this to be true. Inside of us lies a reservoir of untapped potential. There are untold numbers of stories about people who have done amazing feats far exceeding their own expectations. Through insurmountable odds, they were able to rise above defeat, depression, and despondency. They tapped into the potential they were born with in order to live their dreams.

We do not have to think for very long before we come up with the names of those who shattered the barriers of limitations.

The most naturally gifted athlete the world has ever seen, Usain St Leo Bolt, confirmed his tremendous talents when he realized his dreams by winning a phenomenal three gold medals and breaking three world records at the 2008 Olympic Games in Beijing, China. Bolt became the first man in Olympic history to win both the 100m and 200m races in world record times, and as part of the 4x100m team that also smashed the world record. He made history again and became a legend at the 2012 Olympic Games in London by defending all three Olympic titles with 100m, 200m, and 4x100m victories, the latter in a new world record time of 36.84 seconds. Born in 1986 on the island of Jamaica on the rural north coast, he grew up poor. His parents ran a grocery store selling bottles of rum and cigarettes. By the age of twelve, Bolt was the school's fastest 100m sprinter. Now he is a three-time Olympic gold medalist.

Barack Obama made history when he became the first African-American president despite the many naysayers who said that it was impossible for him to win the election. This is not a political statement—just a fact.

Madam C.J. Walker became the first African-American female millionaire who said, "I am a woman who came from the cotton fields of the South. From there I was promoted to the washtub. From there I was promoted to the cook kitchen. From there I promoted myself into the business of manufacturing hair goods and preparations....I have built my own factory on my own ground."[1]

Kathryn Kuhlman's unique abilities to yield to the power of the Holy Spirit and the untapped potential inside of her, enabled her to see thousands of people healed from all kinds of diseases.

These people all had one thing in common—they believed they could achieve their goal. They believed that as they yielded themselves to God, they would do great things. They also disciplined themselves and did the work necessary to achieve their goals. It takes strategy, commitment, and dedication to accomplish big goals.

> *But without faith it is impossible to please him: for he that cometh to God must believe that he is, and that he is a rewarder of them that diligently seek him.*
> *(Hebrews 11:6)*

Between potential and greatness, however, there are challenges—circumstances and situations that threaten

---

1. Madam Walker, National Negro Business League Convention, July 1912

to keep us from becoming all that we were created to be.

We live in a world where boundaries are all around us—where people are constantly telling us what we are capable or incapable of doing. They say things like, "It has never been done before" or "No one has ever done it this way"—"You're too dumb to be a lawyer" or "You're too fat to be a doctor" or "You're too dark; no one wants a dark woman." People are always pushing their self-imposed limitations on others.

If you do not know any better, you will believe their lies. If a person does not know that they were born for a reason and that they were not a "mistake," they muddle through life being kicked around like a football.

Master of Our Fate?

Many people believe that we are the master of our own fate. William Ernest Henley said, "I am the master of my fate: I am the captain of my soul." They believe that whatever circumstances we find ourselves in today are the result of the decisions and choices we have made.

I choose to believe that I am in control of my life. I am responsible for the outcomes of the choices I make. God created me as a free agent—not a robot whose every movement is decided by someone else. However, I also realize that God is sovereign—that He exceeds all authority and power! There are those who use the sovereignty of God as an excuse to not take responsibility for their own decisions—to not use their God-given authority and power to maximize the potential God created them with. "God is in control," they say, as though they do not have to do anything but sit back on autopilot while life rolls along—just sit back and enjoy the ride. I beg to differ with this thought process.

We have been given all power and authority here on earth. We simply have to use it.

We are created in the image of God—filled with unlimited potential that, through the enabler, the Holy Spirit, we can have whatever we believe we can have. There is nothing else that God is going to do. We have been given all power and authority here on earth. We simply have to use it.

That means no matter what situation or circumstances you may find yourself in, you can get through it. You can rise above it. You can beat it. You can win!

For as he thinks in his heart, so is he. (Proverbs 23:7)

In my own personal life I have enjoyed adventures beyond what many people experience simply because I chose to believe.

One evening my husband and I were watching the travel channel. It was a special about a place in South Africa called The Sun City Resort. The resort draws thousands of visitors each year to its four hotels, including two five-star hotels: the Palace of the Lost City (which forms part of The Leading Hotels of the World) and The Cascades Hotel. In the television special, they were showing photos of the Palace of the Lost City hotel—the delectable buffet meals, the lush, beautiful landscape, the exquisite rooms, and all that the hotel had to offer. I was mesmerized. I could see myself there. I envisioned myself sitting at one of the pools relaxing, eating sweet pineapple, and dining on meals fit for a queen.

I said to my husband, "I want to visit there!"

"Impossible," some would say.

Well, within one year we were on our way to South Africa to stay in the Palace of the Lost City. That proved to be one of the best trips that we ever made. It was amazing. When I saw that television show, I immediately grabbed hold of what I saw and what I felt. I believed that I could actually visit that place. The power to create and obtain "wealth" is inside of me so I tapped into my God-given imagination, and saw myself there in that beautiful place where the rich and famous visit.

I could have said, "Oh well, I guess I will never visit that place. We could never afford it." Well, guess what? We did not have to pay to stay there and we did not have to pay to get there. It was an all-expense paid vacation! Go figure! This trip was only one of many exotic vacations our family has taken.

Key Points

- We all possess a strength or a supernatural power within waiting for us to call on it to bring it to the forefront.
- People everywhere are discovering that inside of them is a power which is endless, strength that is resilient, billows of peace waiting to consume them, victory wanting to encapsulate defeat, and possibilities waiting to be called upon.
- We have been given all power and authority here on earth. We simply have to use it.

Discovery Action Steps

The first thing that you must do is enlarge the territory of your mind. Dream bigger! Take the limits off!

What is your dream?

The limitations are only in your mind, in your thinking. I challenge you today to begin a renovation of your mind. Tear down the old-dilapidated frame and structure and start building with a fresh, new foundation—one that can hold the new life-prints you are creating.

For as he thinks in his heart, so is he. (Proverbs 23:7)

List whatever limitations either you or someone else has put on your dream.

Then go through them one by one and change the negative to a positive and cross that limitation off the list.

Remember, if you can believe it, it is possible! God has so much more for you!

Do you believe it? Can you see it? Can you touch it?

CHAPTER 2
Unleashing the Power Within

"Our deepest fear is not that we are inadequate. Our deepest fear is that we are powerful beyond measure. It is our light, not our darkness that most frightens us. We ask ourselves, "Who am I to be brilliant, gorgeous, talented, and fabulous?" Actually, who are you not to be? You are a child of God. Your playing small does not serve the world. There is nothing enlightened about shrinking so that other people will not feel insecure around you. We are all meant to shine. We were born to make manifest the glory of God that is within us. It is not just in some of us; it is in everyone. As we let our own light shine, we unconsciously give other people permission to do the same. As we are liberated from our own fear, our presence automatically liberates others." (Marianne Williamson)

Marianne said a mouth full. She also brings to our minds some very important questions.

Why does our light frighten us?

Why don't we want to shine brightly for everyone to see?

I remember an incident that happened when I was in elementary school. It was my turn to spell a word in the Spelling Bee. Fearful, trembling, and feeling very uncomfortable while standing in front of the whole class, I misspelled the word on purpose so that I would be eliminated from the contest. Why would a child do this? Why didn't I want to show everyone how smart I was, and that I had studied and prepared well?

The answer is easy. I did not want to outshine the other children who had already been disqualified. I did not want to compete with the children who were still in the contest. I did not like being in the limelight. As a child I had also been bullied for being smart, and fear had gripped me. It was easier for me to fade into the crowd than to be singled out and put on display for being smart. I learned at an early age that being the smart kid in class can subject you to unwanted attention.

However, to dumb down and live a mediocre life is of no benefit to anyone. Settling for less than our best is not cool and frankly it does not even make sense. When we live this way we are actually living a lie. When the universe calls for the gifts that we have been given, often we do not answer because we fear our authentic self is the one who is being called. The problem is we have not seen our authentic self for a very long time, if ever. We do not know how to locate him.

Through the Eight-Step Transformation Process I will be introducing to you in this book, I will help you to drill down and find your authentic self. Being who God created you to be is how you are able to unleash the power within.

God the Holy Spirit was sent to us to reside inside of us after Jesus returned to heaven to sit at the right hand of His Father to make intercession for us. The Holy Spirit is now positioned to do the work of the Father in each of our lives. God wants to display His glory in our lives and unleash Himself, and expand each of us to fully embrace who He has created us to be. We need to begin to tap into this power and begin to truly be all that we have been designed to be.

To dumb down and live a mediocre life is of no benefit to anyone.

Acres of Diamonds

An African farmer heard stories of men who made their riches prospecting for diamonds. The farmer decided to sell his farm and join the others prospecting for diamonds. The farmer spent the rest of his short life prospecting for diamonds, never with any success. With nothing to show for his years of work, the farmer ended up committing suicide.

Meanwhile, back at the farm which the now dead farmer once sold, there was a small stream. One day, the man who bought the farm found a stone in a stream on the property. He did not know exactly what it was, but it was nice looking enough that he placed it on his mantle. Soon after placing that stone on the mantle, a visitor saw it and was in shock. Immediately, he asked the man if he knew what he had found.

That stone sitting on the mantle happened to be the largest diamond ever discovered. Better yet, the stream on his farm was filled with similar stones. Turns out, it was the most productive diamond mine in all of Africa.

The moral of the story is pretty easy to see—opportunity, wealth, happiness—whatever you want is right in your own backyard. You are standing in your own acres of diamonds. You just need the patience and persistence to keep searching your own backyard (Russell Conwell).

Right Place at the Right Time

You are exactly where you should be at this moment in time. You may have thought to yourself, *I have blown it, I have missed it and I will never get out of life what I want.* This is a lie and you must not receive it. You have to realize that every decision you have made has lead you to this moment in time. It is now time for you to take your life to another level. Reading this book is not a coincidence. The principles and steps I will give you will help you move your life to a whole new level.

Showing up just as you are right now is part of living the life that you were created to live. If you keep waiting until you are perfect, you will never show up to actively participate in life, you will never be able to go the next level of living.

Infinite Intelligence leads us into all things. I call my higher being God who gives me direction though the Holy Spirit. Some call their higher being by other names. Regardless of what you call your higher power there is someone bigger than you and I calling the shots. You just need to show up fully, originally, and unforgettably ready to unleash the power within.

Being who God created you to be is how you are able to unleash the power within.

Do the Work on You

Make no mistake about it, there is an amazing and wonderful life waiting for us all to take advantage of. However, we have to get ready to receive that life. We have to be watching for clues that reveal the gifts we have been given and how we are to use them. I had one such experience that helped me begin to see what I was called to do with my life.

I was in the house when my brother Lessley called out and said laughingly, "Lynn, Andy is here to see you."

Andy was "slow." He was bullied and made fun of because of his mental challenges. My house was on the way home from his job at McDonalds so he periodically stopped by during the summer months to sit on the porch and talk. I knew that I was called to empower, help, and inspire people to live their best life as I sat on the porch talking with Andy.

I knew that I loved people and that I was called to make an impression on their lives. I also knew that I had to do some work on myself before I could ever see my dreams and desires come to pass. Rejection and feelings of unworthiness had already started to settle in my young teenage mind. Until I became secure in who I was, I could not go on to fulfill what I was seeing I was called to do. Like many of you, I needed to discover the authentic me buried deep inside of me. I needed to do some excavating and find the hidden treasure that was within me.

Excavating You

Merriam-Webster defines excavate, to form a cavity or hole in, to form by hollowing out, and to dig out and remove. The job of an archaeologist is to dig, explore, and to seek to find things that have been hidden for many thousands of years. In archaeology, excavation is the exposure, processing, and recording of archaeological remains. An excavation site or "dig" is a site being studied.

So it is with digging for your authentic self. Rediscovering important components of who you really are will set your feet on a path of healing, wholeness, and destiny. You are a gift to the world waiting to be opened up for the world to see. You are like a drink offering for someone who has been traveling the dry, hot desert. You are not a mirage, you are the real deal.

Though excavating is hard work, it is well worth doing because you will discover a secret treasure that has been covered and hidden for thousands of years. That is why I believe that you are exactly where you should be. It is time to showcase your gifts and talents by serving others.

I was kind of lost in that world of doing what I thought I was supposed to do in the way I was supposed to do it; and to a degree, it worked. But the people I was attracting were coming to me for something other than the most profound gift that I could give. I was on my way, but I had yet to discover the true me. There were too many outside voices trying to tell me who they thought I should be.

Getting to know your own voice can be a daunting task when you hear so many voices. Get the other voices out of your head. Embrace who you are and discover your likes, dislikes, preferences, and differences. Stop apologizing for being who you were created to be.

"A fish cannot drown in water. A bird does not fall in air. Each creature God made must live in its own true nature." (Mechthild of Magdeburg)

There is true vitality that waits beneath all we do that we can tap into if we can discover what we love. If you feel energy, excitement, and a sense that life is happening for the first time, you are probably near unearthing your God-given gifts and talents, and living in your own true nature. Joy in what we do is not an added feature. It is a sign of deep total health.

I developed an acronym for the word stop. This acronym describes what we should do as we are going through the excavation process.

STOP

Settle down - Get quiet in your spirit through meditating, listening to music, exercising or walking. In order to hear, you must be in a state of rest and relaxation.

Trust yourself - Trust that you are hearing correctly, and that you are doing what you should be doing. Get rid of all doubt during the time when you settle yourself. Get the negative voices out of your head.

Observe - Watch and pray. Pay attention. Perceive your surroundings, your feeling, and your thoughts. What are you hearing, thinking about, and experiencing? Is there peace or confusion? Is there bounty or lack? Is there happiness or sadness? Observe and act accordingly.

Proceed - Faith without works is not faith at all. Get moving. Start doing, walking, building—just move forward.

Key Points

To dumb down and live a mediocre life is of no benefit to anyone.

Why does our light frighten us?

Why don't we want to shine brightly for everyone to see?

Being who God created you to be is how you are able to unleash the power within.

> *Do you know who God created you to be?*

> *Are you striving to be that person?*

Discovery Action Steps

Settling for less than your best is not cool and frankly does not even make sense. When you live this way you are actually living a lie.

> *Are you "dumbing down" and living a mediocre life?*

> *Are you settling for and giving less than your best?*

> *Why do you think you are doing that?*

Have you thought to yourself?

> *I have blown it, I have missed it and I will never get out of life what I want.*

This is a lie and you must not receive it. You have to realize that every decision that you have made has lead you to this moment in time. How you chose today will move you into your tomorrow. If you never show up to actively participate in life, you will never be able to go the next level of living. You have to get yourself ready to receive that life.

Are you ready to show up and actively participate in life?

CHAPTER 3
Unlimited Resources

In the beginning, God created the universe. Out of himself came everything. When the earth was as yet unformed and desolate, with the surface of the ocean depths shrouded in darkness, and while the Spirit of God was hovering over the surface of the waters, God spoke and everything come in to being. In the beginning God said let there be light and there was light. He created the world from nothing. He spoke and it was. (Genesis 1:1 ISV)

"God's supply is infinite, with more than enough to meet the demands each of us places upon it." - Kay Haugen, "From the Poorhouse to the Penthouse"

Whatever you need is available to you if you can believe it. Jesus looked at His disciples and said, "With men this is impossible, but all things are possible with God" (Matthew 19:26).

Imagine, God called forth the land and the sea and the fish and the animals, and even you and me. God calls things that are not as though they were. What an amazing thought. Even more amazing is the fact that God has given us this same amazing ability. We can speak and see the manifestation of that which we have spoken. Simply amazing!

> *As it is written, I have made you a father of many nations in the presence of Him whom He believed-God, who gives life to the dead, and calls those things which do not exist as though they did.*
> *(Romans 4:17)*

Calling those things that do not exist as though they did is much like the thermostat in your home. If it is 90 degrees in your home when you arrive from work, and you want it to be a pleasant 75°, you have to set the thermostat on your air conditioner at 75°. When you do that, your thermostat starts calling those things that do not exist as though they did. As long as you leave the thermostat alone, it will continue to call for 75 degrees until the room reaches that temperature.

We must use our words to call for the things that we desire. Where there is lack we must speak abundance, and where there is sorrow we must speak joy. Where there is chaos we must speak order, and where there is hopelessness we must speak hope. There is no lack in God's world, the universe. In the abundant universe, lack does not exist except in our own minds.

Jehovah-Jireh

In both Islamic and Christian religions, there is mentioned of a story about the Prophet Abraham who was asked to sacrifice his son. With fear and trepidation Abraham made his way to Mount Moriah. When he was ready to offer Isaac up as a sacrifice, the angel of the Lord told Abraham not to touch Isaac.

> *"Do not lay a hand on the boy," he said. "Do not do anything to him. Now I know that you fear God, because you have not withheld from me your son, your only son. Abraham looked up and there in a thicket he saw a ram caught by its horns. He went over and took the ram and sacrificed it as a burnt offering instead of his son. So Abraham called that place The* LORD *Will Provide. And to this day it is said, "On the mountain of the* LORD *it will be provided." (Genesis 22:12-14)*

From this passage of scripture comes the name of God, Jehovah-Jireh. The revelation of the name Jehovah-Jireh means the Lord who will see to it that my every need is met because He sees what I need. He is able to meet my need in just the right time as He did for Abraham and meet it fully. Whatever we need, He sees and is able to meet it no matter what it is or how impossible we think it might be.

Science teaches us that for every cause in the universe there is a direct effect. Thought is the cause, reality is the effect. Plainly put, people lack simply because they constantly think about lack. Galatians 6: 7 says, "For whatsoever a man soweth, that shall he also reap" (KJV). This scripture represents the universal Law of Cause and Effect. It is a law which works much like the Law of Gravity does, impersonally and whether we believe in it or not.

A highly cryptic law, the Law of Cause and Effect refers to the fact that we are responsible for the effects of our actions, and that these effects may only begin to be realized as one awakens to their higher nature. It is a reversal of the victim ideology of being subject to the random forces of the universe—an ideology imposed upon us by society and the powers that be—that we have no control over our reality.

"Essentially the Law of Cause and Effect refers to the fact that there are elastic forces within the universe that affect the way our creations and realities are manifested. The complex nature of the reality in which we live is that we have the interaction of individual realities creating a scenario in which our intentions and manifestations as individuals must first interact with the world/universe before being processed and expressed into their final form. Also these intentions and manifestations must be processed by our own conditioned mind which exhibits its own unique distortions and effects upon the original thought." - Law Interpreted by Cosmic Awareness via Will Berlinghoff[2]

---

2. Law Interpreted by Cosmic Awareness via Will Berlinghoff

Science teaches us that for every cause in the universe there is a direct effect. Thought is the cause, reality is the effect.

It matters not whether you are Christian, Muslim, or Atheist, it works the same for everyone at all times. There are no pre-determinations taking place regarding whether the thoughts you provide now will or will not be harmful to you when they ultimately come to pass.

If we lack anything it is because we have not asked and prepared ourselves to receive it. "You have not because you ask not" (James 4:2 NIV).

For as he thinks in his heart, so is he. (Proverbs 23:7)

There are many forms of an abundant life which include joy, laughter, fun, adventure, courage, strength, and peace.

Summing it all up, friends, I would say you will do best by filling your minds and meditating on things true, noble, reputable, authentic, compelling, gracious—the best, not the worst; the beautiful, not the ugly; things to praise, not things to curse. (Philippians 4:8 MSG)

As we continue this journey of life, you will discover how to take advantage of God's unlimited resources and power. Our Eight-Step Transformational Process will lead you down a path where you will be able to learn how to leverage your words, actions, and thoughts.

It was not until I left home to attend college that I truly understood that unlimited possibilities and resources were waiting for me. I grew up in church, attended every Sunday, and loved every minute of it, but there were some things missing in my life. My dad was a hardworking man who was employed in a factory Monday through Friday. He was also a pastor, and on the weekends he performed his pastoral duties of attending to his congregation and preaching. Hearing the gospel message of salvation was very common in our church.

As a student at Western Michigan University, I joined another church and was exposed to teaching from the Bible that I had never encountered. This is where I learned about God's infinite supply of resources. I was never really skeptical or doubtful of what I was learning about this vast reservoir of unlimited resources, all I wanted to know was how do I get it. If that is where you are, continue on with this book.

Key Points

"God's supply is infinite, with more than enough to meet the demands each of us places upon it." - Kay Haugen, "From the Poorhouse to the Penthouse"

Are you ready to experience this abundance in your own life?

Science teaches us that for every cause in the universe there is a direct effect. Thought is the cause, reality is the effect.

> *How is this truth going to affect the way you think from now on?*

Discovery Action Steps

There are many forms of an abundant life which include joy, laughter, fun, adventure, courage, strength, and peace.

> *Are you living an abundant life?*
>
> *Why or why not?*

Read James 4:2.

> *What do you need to start to do?*

Asked yourself:

> *How do I change my current situation or circumstances?*
>
> *How do I leave lack and poverty and move to abundance and prosperity?*
>
> *If there is such a tremendous supply of wealth, why don't I have any?*
>
> *Can all of this be possible?*

Keep on reading and I will tell you what I have discovered.

CHAPTER 4
Make a Decision

"The most difficult thing is the decision to act, the rest is merely tenacity. The fears are paper tigers. You can do anything you decide to do. You can act to change and control your life; and the procedure, the process is its own reward." - Amelia Earhart

For truly, let not such a person imagine that he will receive anything [he asks for] from the Lord, [For being as he is] a man of two minds (hesitating, dubious, irresolute), [he is] unstable and unreliable and uncertain about everything [he thinks, feels, decides]. (James 1:7-9 AMP)

The one simple act of making a decision is very challenging for many people. It is hard to make a choice. You can spend a life time being indecisive, bouncing between, yes and no, go and stay, get married or stay single, start a business or stay at a traditional job, and the list goes on and on. Not to make a decision is like being dangled or suspended in time with no direction and no purpose. You feel hopeless because you are not following a plan or moving forward.

Not making a decision means that you are not making any progress, you are not moving forward. For some, the very thought of making a decision is paralyzing. Actually to not make is decision is making a decision.

The decision-making process involves the following steps:

1. Define the problem or situation.
2. Identify all choices or options.
3. Develop all choices and options.
4. Analyze the choices and options.
5. Select the best choice or option.
6. Implement the decision.
7. Establish a control and evaluation system of your choice.

"Once you make a decision, the universe conspires to make it happen." - Ralph Waldo Emerson

In 2013 I found myself very frustrated with the amount of weight that I had gained over a ten year time span. I was diagnosed with Hypothyroidism several years ago and losing weight for me was nearly impossible. I tried every kind of weight loss product that you can think of. Each time I found a product I did my due diligence and investigated it exhaustively. I read reviews, the ingredients, and looked for product testimonials. All to no avail! I was met time and time again with disappointment and failure.

So imagine the doubt that came over me when I was introduced to yet another weight loss program. For three months I followed two women's weight loss testimonies online. One of them had a YouTube channel with videos chronicling her weight loss journey. I further investigated by speaking to each one of them and asking them questions that I had about the program. To my delight both of them were friendly and forthright about how the weight loss program worked for then.

After months of deliberating, I made the decision to try the program, feeling that it was the best option for me. I was very desperate by then. This decision was not without great fear and trepidation because of my past failures and disappointments with weight loss programs. I placed my order and decided to start in October of 2013. Within a couple of day the weight started dropping off and the inches were melting. I was overjoyed. I was in complete shock. I knew that I had made the right decision. My willingness to make a decision has led several hundred people to also start this weight loss program and see fantastic results. One of my clients lost 100 pounds in ten months. This is all because I made a decision.

Nick Vujicic

Nick Vujicic was born in Australia without limbs due to a rare congenital condition called tetra-amelia syndrome. According to an article in the Daily Mail, when he was born, his dad ran out and vomited, and his mother did not hold him until he was four months old. Bullied and picked on as a child, Nick grew weary and thought that killing himself was the only way out. He tried to drown himself three times without success. The last time he tried to take his life, he saw in his mind's eye the distraught faces of his family members who would be so grieved if they lost him. This affected him greatly so he decided to stop trying to die and to start living.

Jeremiah 29:11, "'For I know the plans I have for you,' declares the Lord, 'plans to prosper you and not to harm you, plans to give you hope and a future,'" was the scripture that Nick hung on to and it became his mantra in life.

If anyone could have felt sorry for themselves it was Nick, but he came to grips with the fact that God had created him for a reason and a purpose. Nick made a decision to live. Today he travels the world inspiring and encouraging others to live their lives to the fullest.

Why don't we like to make decisions?

Through a non-scientific survey on Facebook, I asked my friends why they felt making decisions for some was such a challenge.

Anna Cooks said, "Wanting to please someone or not disappoint someone, self-sabotage (rooted in a lack of confidence and value for self), apathy, no endurance for the process (would rather avoid it then deal with it), immaturity, or fear of change."

Ursula van Stavel shared, "Insecurity, low self-image, and emotional or psychological paralysis."

Jeanette Clark commented, "Laziness and the fear of work is an issue we must address."

Apostle Nina-Marie observed, "Many people fear making major decisions because they are not certain of the outcome. Also they care too much what other people think. Lack of love is always a part of the rejection of change. It involves identity and self-love or the absence thereof."

Ayana D. King added, "The wrong decision may be irreversible."

James Ervin Berry shared, "Fear of failure is probably the biggest reason I can think of. Some would say it is a lack of faith."

Sandra Ratney Griffin wrote, "I believe the #1 reason is fear, a lack of courage, and a lack of trust or confidence in God."

Nadine Cook observed, "Perfectionists tend to procrastinate out of fear of being less than perfect."

Stacy McKinney-Williams said, "I think we worry too much about what others will think or say (behind our backs) if we are not successful in the decisions that we make. We sometimes let what other people think of us, consume and control our decisions to take that big leap."

Faith Larkins commented, "We become comfortable in the skin that we are in so when change approaches, we back away. It is in the realization that change is good and refreshing that we release the old (that was not working anyway) and embrace the newness of God.

Each of my Facebook friends shared a different reason that they feel making decisions in challenging for some. What is your reason for hesitating to make decision?

Key Points

"The most difficult thing is the decision to act, the rest is merely tenacity. The fears are paper tigers. You can do anything you decide to do. You can act to change and control your life; and the procedure, the process is its own reward." - Amelia Earhart

"Once you make a decision, the universe conspires to make it happen." - Ralph Waldo Emerson

Discovery Action Steps

The decision making process involves the following steps. Check them off as you strive to become a more effective and consistent decision maker.

1. Define the problem or situation.
2. Identify all choices or options.
3. Develop all choices and options.
4. Analyze the choices and options.
5. Select the best choice or option.
6. Implement the decision.
7. Establish a control and evaluation system of your choice.

CHAPTER 5
Discovering Your Authentic Self

What is your answer when you are asked, "Who are you?" Do you say, "I am a mom," "I am a doctor," or "I live in Ohio"? Often the answer is not who you are, but what you do, what your social status is, or how you see your function in life. You cannot answer who you are because you do not really know.

There is another level of existence that is the real, true, and genuine substance of who you are. It is what Dr. Phil defines as the authentic self.

"The authentic self is the you that can be found at your absolute core. It is the part of you not defined by your job, function or role. It is the composite of all your skills, talents, and wisdom. It is all of the things that are uniquely yours and need expression, rather than what you believe you are supposed to be and do."
- Dr. Phil

Finding Your Authentic Voice

Let me tell you a story about a woman named Antoinette Tuff who found her authentic voice when she was faced with a life or death situation.

It was a school day like any other until a man with an AK-47 type weapon slipped into Ronald E. McNair Discovery Learning Academy and fired shots into the ground. Antoinette sprang into action. The bookkeeper and eight-year veteran of the DeKalb County Georgia School District called 911 from the school's office. Then she worked as go-between communicating with the shooter and the police dispatcher during a tense thirty-one-minute confrontation, eventually talking the suspect into surrendering.

Here is some of the dialogue from the transcript between Tuff, the 911 Dispatcher, and the suspect. Due to the length of the transcript I have eliminated some of it, but left enough to keep the conversation in proper context and to make some very important observations.

Tuff: I am on Second Avenue in the school and the gentleman said tell them to hold down the police officers that are coming or he is going to start shooting so tell them to back off.

Dispatcher: One moment.

Tuff: Do not let anyone in the building, including the police.

Dispatcher: Okay, stay on the line with me, ma'am. Where are you?

Tuff: I am in the front office. (gunshots) Oh, he just went outside and started shooting. (gunshots) Can I run?

Dispatcher: (gunshots) Can you get somewhere safe?

Tuff: Yeah, I got to go. He going to see me running. He coming back.

Tuff: He said he should have went to the mental hospital instead of doing this because he is not on his medication.

Dispatcher: Okay.

Tuff: (to the suspect) I can help you. Do you want to talk to them? Okay. Well let me talk to them and let's see if we can work it out so you don't have to go away with them for a long time. No, it does matter. I can let them know that you have not tried to harm me or do anything with me or anything. (to the dispatcher) Let me ask you this, ma'am. He didn't hit anybody he just shot outside the door, if I walk out there with him so they won't shoot him or anything like that. He wants to give himself up. Is that okay? They won't shoot him?

Dispatcher: Yes, ma'am.

Tuff: He wants to go to the hospital.

Dispatcher: Okay.

Tuff: (to the suspect) She said hold on and she going to talk to the police officer and I'll go out there with you. Well, don't feel bad, baby. My husband just left me after thirty-three years. I mean, I'm sitting here with you and talking to you about it. I got a son that's multiple disabled. It's all going to be well. They are just going to talk to the police. **I love you.**

Tuff: Tell the officers don't come in shooting and tell them to come on in. I'll buzz them in.

Dispatcher: Okay.

Tuff: Hold on. Sit there and I'll buzz them in so you know when they coming. Okay? Stay there calm. Don't worry about it. I'll sit here so they see you not trying to harm me. Okay?

Dispatcher: Okay

Tuff: It's going to be all right, sweetie. I want you to know I love you, okay? I'm proud of you. That's a good thing you're giving up and don't worry about it. We all go through something in life. No, you don't want that. You going to be okay. It's going to be all right. Sweetheart. I want you to know I love you. You going to be okay. I thought the same thing, you know. I tried to commit suicide last year after my husband left me, but look at me now. I'm still working and everything is ok.

Tuff: They are coming. So just hold on, Michael. Go ahead and lay down. Go ahead and lay down. You just got your phone? Okay. That's fine. Tell them to come on. Come on. He just got his phone. That's all he got is his phone.

Tuff: (to dispatcher) Let me tell you something, baby, nothing so scary in my life.

Dispatcher: Me, either. But you did great.

Tuff: Oh, Jesus. Oh, God.

This story caught national attention in light of the shootings that have taken place in some of our schools in America. Antoinette was a hero. She found her authentic voice even through the pain that she was encountering in her own life. She said three things during this ordeal that stuck out: "I can help you, I love you, and I'm proud of you." Authenticity comes from a place of love. It is at the core of your being. People know when you genuinely care about them and want to help them.

Mariah Carey sings a song titled Hero. The chorus says, "And then a hero comes along, with the strength to carry on. And you cast your fears aside. And you know you can survive. So when you feel like hope is gone. Look inside you and be strong. And you'll finally see the truth. That a hero lies in you."

Authenticity comes from a place of love.

Discovering Your Authentic Self

"To be yourself in a world that is constantly trying to make you something else is the greatest accomplishment." - Ralph Waldo Emerson

Nina Siegal of the New York Times wrote a story about a painting titled "Sunset at Montjajour," which had been considered a fake and stored in an attic private collection. It has now been proven by the Van Gogh Museum that the work is a genuine product of the master painter, Van Gogh.

"How could 'Sunset at Montjajour' be considered a fake when it was indeed painted by the great Van Gogh? As rare as it may be, original paintings do surface occasionally. Louis van Tilborgh, the museum's senior researcher, said that since 1991, the museum has developed several new techniques for identifying and authenticating works of art. He said that all those methods were put to use when researchers had the chance to look at this painting again.

According to Mr. Van Tilborgh, it was painted on the same type of canvas with the same type of underpainting Van Gogh used for at least one other painting of the same area, "The Rocks." The work was also listed as part of Theo van Gogh's collection in 1890. It has "180'" painted on the back, which corresponds to the number in the collection inventory. "That was the clincher," he said then added. "This time, we have topographical information, plus a number of other factors that have helped us to establish authenticity. Research is so much more advanced now; so, we could come to a very different conclusion."

Thank God it is not quite as hard to discover our authenticity. It may take a little while, but when you go to the master creator He can validate that He created you and what He created you for.

Dark Girls

If you are one of the lucky ones who has already discovered your authentic self, you are well on your way to living the life of service that you were born to live. You are way ahead of the game. Most of us spend years of self-discovery. The world we live in has a way of defining who we are, what we can do, and when we cannot do it. The world has a way of shaping us based on various criteria such as our educational level, our race, our size, our gender, and our financial status in the world. Within each of the criteria mentioned there are sub criteria. For example within the Black American community there are varying shades of skin. Some say the darker the skin tone the more prejudice a person experiences.

I watched a documentary titled "Dark Girls." This was a world television documentary presented on the Oprah Winfrey Network, which explored the deep-seated biases and attitudes about skin color, particularly dark skinned women, outside and within the Black American culture. This fascinating and controversial documentary film goes beneath the surface to explore the prejudices that dark-skinned women face throughout the world. It explores the roots of classism, racism, and the lack of self-esteem within a segment of culture that spans from America to the most remote corners of the globe. Women shared their personal stories, touching on the deeply ingrained beliefs and attitudes of society, while allowing generations to heal as they learned to love themselves for who they are.

There were mixed emotions about "Dark Girls." Some people were clueless to the fact that Black women encounter a greater level of challenges because they are darker. I guess they thought that when Dr. Martin Luther King, Jr. said about looking for a day when people would be judged less by the color of their skin than by the content of their character that he was just making a baseless or somewhat exaggerated speech. When Dr. King made this statement I am sure he was not referring to prejudice based on skin tone among his own race.

This documentary shows just one of the ways society and culture tries to tell us who we are. It is imperative that we discover our authentic self. We must learn the reason that we were born! If we do not get to our grass-root self, we will be knocked off of our spot and will never live the life we were created to live.

Only Your Authentic Self Can Fulfill the Call

There is a "tribe" of people you were called to serve. The way that you attract them is by being authentically you. Everything that you do has to come from a place of love. How you present yourself, how you connect, and how you speak convey your level of love. It all has to be in alignment with your heart, your truth, your vision, and your message. The message cannot be from a place of ego, fear, competition or of trying to fit in by wearing a mask or pretending to be someone other than yourself.

Love flows from the river of authenticity.

In the Bible it is said that the followers of Jesus recognize His voice and that they will not follow a stranger's voice. When Judith Fain was a Ph.D. candidate at the University of Durham, she spent several months each year in Israel as part of her studies. One day while walking on a road near Bethlehem, Judith watched as three shepherds converged with their separate flocks of sheep. The three men hailed each other and then stopped to talk. While they were conversing, their sheep intermingled, melting into one big flock.

Wondering how the three shepherds would ever be able to identify their own sheep, Judith waited until the men were ready to say their good-byes. She watched, fascinated, as each of the shepherds called out to his sheep. At the sound of their shepherd's voice, like magic, the sheep separated again into three flocks. Apparently some things in Israel have not changed for thousands of years.

The same must be said of you. Whose voice will you follow? When you opt to work outside of your authentic self, you attract a people whose needs you cannot address. They come to you in search of a gift that you do not have to give. Being authentic enables you to serve with gladness and joy and not sadness and sorrow.

Key Points

"The authentic self is the you that can be found at your absolute core. It is the part of you not defined by your job, function or role. It is the composite of all your skills, talents, and wisdom. It is all of the things that are uniquely yours and need expression, rather than what you believe you are supposed to be and do." - Dr. Phil

Authenticity comes from a place of love.

"To be yourself in a world that is constantly trying to make you something else is the greatest accomplishment." (Ralph Waldo Emerson)

Love flows from the river of authenticity.

Discovery Action Steps

Finding your authentic self can take years. It is a process that requires commitment, tenacity, dedication, and wherewithal. Finding your authentic self is like excavating a diamond mine. Start by answering these questions.

- *What is you answer when you are asked, "Who are you"?*
- *Whose voice have you been following?*
- *Have you been serving with gladness and joy or sadness and sorrow?*
- *Do you know the reason you were born?*

CHAPTER 6
Rule Your World

"O Divine Providence, I ask not for more riches but more wisdom with which to make wiser use of the riches you gave me at birth, consisting in the power to control and direct my own mind to whatever ends I might desire." - Napoleon Hill

Do you believe that you are where you are today because of the choices and decisions that you have made?

Do you believe that the choices that you are making today will determine where you find yourself tomorrow and in your future?

You have been given authority to rule your world. You were created with the capacity to make decisions. You are powerful. You can create the kind of world that you want to experience. If you are sad you can make yourself happy. If you are broke you have the power to create wealth. Your dreams can become a reality through the choices that you make. Where you are today is a consequence of the choices and decisions that you have made. If you are happy with where you are, keep making decisions the way that you have. If you know that there is more for you to do, new places to visit, others to empower, and new doors to walk through, read on because it is time to really take your world to another dimension.

Where you are today is a consequence of the choices and decisions that you have made.

Dominion

Dominion is a topic that many of us talk about, but few of us really possess. Dominion in its simplest form is power, authority or control over something or someone. It is the ability to request or command and expect a fulfillment of that appeal. To have dominion is to rule and to be in charge. Dominion is understanding that you can do what God said you can do, have what God said you can have, and be what God said you can be regardless of what things look like, seem like, sound like or appear like.

> *What is man, that you are mindful of him? And the son of man, that thou visitest him? For you have made him (man) a little lower than the angels, and have crowned him with glory and honor. You made him (man) to have dominion over the works of your hands; you have put all things under his feet. (Psalm 8:4-6 KJV)*

It is amazing to think that we have been created in the image of God and that we were made a little lower than the angels. Can you fathom that? Can you wrap your mind around this thought? Angels are very powerful beings who do the bidding of God. He tells them where to go and what to do. They are spirit beings who live to enforce the thoughts and ideas of God.

With this in mind you can say that humans are powerful and have great authority. Being made a little lower than angels and in the image of God means that we are created to delve deeper and climb higher to grasp this great potential that resides within us.

Isn't it time to take your rightful place in the world and take dominion? Nothing more will be done for you. You are in charge. However, you are not alone in trying to figure all of this out! You do not have to rely on your own understanding or your own comprehension. There is a power greater than you and I who is here to help.

Infinite Intelligence

Man is created in the image of God and is a triune being which consists of body, spirit, and soul. Our spirit lives in a body and has a soul. We have a spiritual nature that is separate and distinct from the body in which it dwells. It is the spirit of man who connects with Infinite Intelligence or the Holy Spirit, as Christians refer to Him.

The Holy Spirit is the power source. He is available to everyone who calls upon Him. To help with this concept, think of how many ways the power of electricity is used. With it people light their cities, cook, heat their homes, run their factories, and operate all kinds of machinery. Men have learned how to use electric power so they can do what used to seem impossible, even go to the moon. However, nothing works unless we connect to the power source.

The Holy Spirit wants to fill your life with a power greater than electricity—power to do what is impossible without it. However, you must connect to it and learn to use it. Used in the right way, this power will bring glory to God and blessing to your life. Power of any kind used in the wrong way will always bring trouble.

The best way to describe Infinite Intelligence is to think of all the energy that exists in the universe being a single entity and that entity being in total communication with every aspect of itself. It thus contains the sum knowledge of the entire universe, from the immense power of the mighty stars to the humblest single cell life form. Yet this energy is almost ethereal in nature, being invisible to our physical senses and only measurable with the most sensitive and advanced instruments that we can produce and then only in rudimentary form.

Access to such knowledge can only be obtained by a similarly ethereal link, but each of us possesses that link. Most of us just do not know it. Those of us who comprehend its existence as far as we are able, are learning how to access it via our mental link and have created amazing things to date. But these things are material and barely scratch the surface of what is believed to be possible.

We live in physical bodies and correspond to the material realm, so it is only natural that we should create on the material plane. The Carnegies, Edisons,

Rockefellers, Wrights, Shakespears, Lincolns, Da Vinci's, Dickens, etc. were all of this world and tapped into this power. They produced incredible results in the creation of wealth, power, invention, art, and a thousand and one other things that have enriched their lives and the lives of millions on the material plane of this life.

"One day, we will progress and unravel more secrets, but for now it is enough to have faith and simply accept the existence of such a power." - Meher Baba

THE HOLY SPIRIT IS THE SOURCE OF THIS POWER AND OUR CONNECTION TO INFINITE INTELLIGENCE. He was sent for the purpose of leading, guiding, directing, and teaching us. "When the Spirit of truth comes," Jesus said, "He will lead you into all truth" (John 16:13).

The "big secret" that seems to be hidden from the masses is that anyone can access Infinite Intelligence.

Accessing Infinite Intelligence

The "big secret" that seems to be hidden from the masses is that anyone can access Infinite Intelligence. It is not really hidden at all because it can be done by connecting and submitting ourselves to the working of the Holy Spirit in our lives. We have to yield. We must quiet our minds from the business of the day so that we can receive from Holy Spirit on a regular basis. We must do this daily because we are depleted of this power when we interact with people in the world. No need to fear though because the supply of power from the Holy Spirit never ends.

However, the mind needs to be still and receptive to the ideas and "hunches" that come to it. When we ask for answers to problems that beset us or need to know how to achieve or create something in our lives, we need to know how to ask the right question in the right way!

We do this by forming a definite go all the way to they are simply or desire in our mind. The best way to do that is to physically write it down! When you see the thing you want there in front of you in black and white, it fixes the desire in your mind. This enables your thoughts to dwell on that desire over and over to the point where it becomes affixed in the subconscious part of your mind as a definite major purpose or desire in your life.

It is no good simply wanting to be rich or to live in a peaceful world because these are not definite desires. These are indefinite and the general desires of the masses which is why they do not come into form. They are simply not asked for in the right way.

To illicit a definite answer, you must ask a definite question!

By creating a subconscious knowledge of the definite thing you desire, your conscious mind will put your desire before the Holy Spirit and access Infinite Intelligence. Then your questions will be answered in a manner you can act upon whether it is a specific idea or a hunch. It is then up to you to recognize an answer when it is given to you. Many do not and blindly dismiss these fleeting "hunches" as of little or no value.

This is where the masses go wrong! When you have created a definite purpose, a solid desire for a thing and you receive those hints as to how you may achieve the thing desired, you have to accept the idea and act upon it! If you do not then you will have missed out on what could potentially alter your life for the better.

Infinite Intelligence from the Holy Spirit is here to help you with anything and everything that you need help with. Do not be shy, ask and you shall receive.

Here are seven steps that will help you start ruling your world.

1. Make your own choices. Take responsibility for your own life. Own your choices. Use your mind.
2. Ask for help from the Holy Spirit and receive Infinite Intelligence.
3. Be who **you** are, not what somebody else tries to make you. Ask yourself, who am I and what do I want? Hone in on you. Lean into who God made you to be.
4. Form your own opinions. Do not be swayed by popular opinion.
5. Do not let anyone make you feel powerless, you can always do something. Do not give your power away.

No one can make you do or feel unless you allow them to.

6. Stand up for what you believe in. If you do not stand for something you will fall for anything.

7. Live your life the way you want to! If you do not follow **your** own path and discover **your** own truth, you will never be able to control **your** world and succeed with **your** goal.

I realized early in life that there were things that I could control. There were things that I could plan and see materialize, and ideas and thoughts that I could see manifested. It takes persistence and a plan. It takes belief that you can have what you are asking for, and it also takes diligence. You cannot play by the same rules as everyone else and expect extraordinary results.

Steve Scott said, "People who achieve ordinary outcomes do so by using conventional approaches and methods taught in schools and used by the masses. People who achieve extraordinary-to-near impossible outcomes do so by using a different set of Master Strategies that are universally and consistently used by Super Achievers. These are virtually unknown to the masses."

We each have the power within to manifest the kind of life we want. Through the Eight-step Transformation Process we will give later in this book, you can achieve an extraordinary abundant life.

I could never possibly accomplish all of the goals and dreams that I have in this lifetime. There have, however, been many goals and dreams that have been attained, and for that I am grateful. I live in a nice home, have a great family, a terrific husband I have been married for over thirty-three years. I have travelled the world, and have owned several successful small businesses. I have enjoyed serving the world in various capacities—yet I know there is more. I am nowhere near finished. I have some **big** dreams and goals that I want to see fulfilled. The question of course is how.

A Life GPS System

The key to success is learning how to rule your world. Ruling your world requires you to strategize and come up with a plan. Deborah the prophet did it. Queen Esther did it. Condoleezza did it and Oprah did it, too! I am not, by any means, holding myself in the same regard as these great women who have achieved so much. What I am saying is that in order to accomplish any goal or dream I need a plan, a strategy, a blueprint, if you will—a roadmap. I need a life GPS system.

Whenever our family travels and we rent a car in a foreign city or state, I enjoy having a GPS system as it keeps us from getting lost and saves us a lot of time, frustration, and wasted energy. These very technical geographical devices are absolutely amazing in how they can track where we are and get us where we are trying to go. According to the manual that comes with one of the popular GPS systems it will give turn-by-turn voice guidance and upgradeable, real-time traffic alerts. Why would we ever leave home without one?

Why then do we wander through life without any plans or thoughts of where we are going? When we go on vacation, we will sit and plan with great detail where we are going, how we are going to get there, what we are going to do when we get there, and where we will stay. It would seem to me that even more energy should be put into writing our life plans. So how do we get this Life GPS System we obviously need?

We know that God has plans for our lives that are good and wonderful. However, our Father wants to engage and actually have us interact with Him as He leads and directs us towards our destiny. Each one of us has the capacity to do more than we think we can. We can live better, healthier, and more successful lives if we would just do things a little bit differently. Many times we limit ourselves because of fear, ignorance, and laziness. God is saying we already have the potential within us, we just need to plug into the power source.

I love watching the show, the Big Idea. "The Big Idea" is a roadmap to the American Dream. Each weeknight, Donny Deutsch, the maverick CEO who built a multi-billion dollar advertising and media business, introduces viewers to the men and women who have made **billions** with their Big Idea. Whether it is a one-on-one with Bill

Gates, a special American Dream series town hall meeting with John Paul Dejoria, or just the average entrepreneur next door who became a millionaire, the same questions can be asked. "What did they do that I have not done? What do they know that I do not know? Why not me?" The secrets of their successes can make you rich. They are ruling their individual worlds.

When I watch this show, I realize that the capacity to dominate lies within me—that God has fearfully and wonderfully made me in His image. I have not begun to tap into the power that resides in me. The same is true for you. There is so much more for you to do! Your best is yet to come. Do not allow your past to dictate your future. Do not hit the brakes. It is time to roll out and get started. Momentum is building and things are getting ready to take off. Do not miss your flight! Plug into the power source of your Life GPS System and download all the data you need to get there!

Key Points

Where you are today is a consequence of the choices and decisions that you have made.

To illicit a definite answer, you must ask a definite question!

Infinite Intelligence is here to help you with anything and everything that you need help with.

Do not be shy, ask and you shall receive.

The "big secret" that seems to be hidden from the masses is that anyone can access Infinite Intelligence.

Steve Scott said, "People who achieve ordinary outcomes do so by using conventional approaches and methods taught in schools and used by the masses. People who achieve extraordinary-to-near impossible outcomes do so by using a different set of Master Strategies that are universally and consistently used by Super Achievers. These are virtually unknown to the masses."

Your best is yet to come. Do not allow your past to dictate your future

Discovery Action Steps

Do you believe that you are where you are today because of the choices and decisions that you have made? _____ Explain your answer:

Do you believe that the choices that you are making today will determine where you find yourself tomorrow and in your future? _____ Why or why not?

Dominion is understanding that you can do what God said you can do, have what God said you can have, and be what God said you can be regardless to what things look like, seem like, sound or appear like to our natural senses.

If you are happy with where you are, keep making decisions the way that you have. If not, review these steps to ruling your world. Check off the ones you are doing.

Circle the ones you need to work on and then list some ways you are going to begin.

1. Make your own choices. Take responsibility for your own life. Own your choices. Use your mind.

2. Ask for help from Infinite Intelligence.

3. Be who **you** are, not what somebody else tries to make you. Ask yourself, who am I and what do I want? Hone in to the real you. Lean in.

4. Form your own opinions. Do not be swayed by popular opinion.

5. Do not let anyone make you feel powerless, you can always do something.

    Do not give your power away. No one can make you think or feel unless you allow them to.

6. Stand up for what you believe in. If you do not stand for something you will fall for anything.

7. Live your life the way you want to! If you do not follow **your** own path and discover **your** own truth, you will never be able to control **your** world and succeed with **your** goal.

Do not hit the brakes. It is time to roll out and get started. Momentum is building and things are getting ready to take off. Do not miss your flight! Plug into the power source of your Life GPS System and download all the data you need to get there!

CHAPTER 7
Overcoming Obstacles

"If you are trying to achieve, there will be roadblocks. I have had them; everybody has had them. However, obstacles do not have to stop you. If you run into a wall, do not turn around and give up. Figure out how to climb it, go through it, or work around it." - Michael Jordan

If achieving goals were easy, everyone would do it quickly and without difficulty. Even if your vision is clear and you can articulate a detailed destiny, there are always obstacles in the path. It is the joy and journey of clearing those obstacles that makes life rich, and helps people feel truly accomplished when they finally reach their pinnacle of success.

When a person joins the military they attend Basic Combat Training (BCT). This training includes crawling, climbing, pulling, and jumping their way through an obstacle course. BCT training is necessary because in combat battle conditions cannot be predicted nor can the weather conditions or terrain be predetermined. So they have to prepare for all kinds of situations and challenges.

They climb fences, jump over barrels, roll in the mud and train in the rain, all of this so that they can be as prepared as possible when they come up against any obstacle.

Inc Magazine says that there are three flavors of obstacles.

External Obstacles: These are obstacles outside of your control such as the economy, natural disasters, physical limitations, and the political climate.

Internal Obstacles: These obstacles are generally one-time issues, but you have direct control over them, such as debt, cash flow, time availability, needed skills or talent.

Habitual Obstacles: These obstacles reflect how people get in their own way. They can only be removed with behavioral change.

Kevin Daum, best-selling author, writes that to overcome obstacles business or personal, you must master these areas:

1. Embrace Self-Awareness
2. Use Time to Your Advantage
3. Commit to Focused Discipline
4. Engage Your Own Creativity

Confidence

Keith Johnson, America's Number one Confidence Coach, says in his book titled, "The Confidence Solution," there is a three-step process that will help you reset your mind-set so that you can function in your peak confidence state.

Step 1-Build Mental Toughness: It is important to think about improving your mental programming. Living at your peak begins in your mind. It all starts with what and how you think. The most powerful muscle in changing the body is the mind.

Step 2-Take Care of Your Emotions and Feelings: Your thoughts and beliefs create your feelings, whether positive or negative, depending on how you were thinking.

Step 3- Change Your Actions and Behavior: Your behavior is tied to your mental and emotional states. Your E-motions are what sets things "IN-motions. If you do not feel confident, you will not act confidently. If you start thinking confidently, you will start feeling confident. When you start thinking and feeling confident, you will start acting confidently. When you start acting confidently, you will consistently perform at your peak performance. When you perform at your peak performance, you will enjoy the thrills of success.

There is a Russian proverb which says, "I cried because I had no shoes until I saw a man who had no feet."

Moses had a stuttering problem, but that did not change God's mind concerning the assignment that he had for Moses. He was given instructions by the Lord to go the pharaoh and tell him that he must allow the children of Israel to go free from bondage. This is what Moses said to the Lord, "Pardon your servant, Lord. I have never been eloquent, neither in the past nor since you have spoken to your servant. I am slow of speech and tongue" (Exodus 4:10).

As if the Lord did not know this about Moses! If your assignment is to give someone a message or to speak in front of a group, do not allow your lack of experience in public speaking or your lack of eloquence in speaking be the obstacle that prevents you from completing your assignment.

> *"I am the LORD your God, who brought you up out of Egypt. Open wide your mouth and I will fill it."*
> *(Psalm 81:10)*

When faced with a bump in the road, sometimes we forget we have a choice: overcome the obstacle or let it overcome you.

Steven Claunch, who was born without fingers on his right hand and with one leg shorter than the other, has excelled in basketball. He explains why obstacles can provide an opportunity to both inspire others and develop character. He says, "There is no dishonor in being born with a disability."

Becky Curran is a twenty-seven-year-old woman who was born an achondroplastic dwarf. This means that she has an average height torso, but shorter arms and legs. She stands 4 feet tall. Every day she is forced to adapt to the "average" height world that she lives in.

Dwarfism is a recognized condition under the Americans with Disabilities Act, but a large number of people with disabilities will tell you that they would not change anything except for how the world reacts to their disability. That is a mouthful.

There are an estimated 30,000 people in the United States living with one of the 200 forms of dwarfism. Dwarfs only represent 0.02 percent of the U.S. population, which means that most little people encounter at least one person each day who has never seen one before. It is not uncommon for these people to stare and occasionally laugh when they first see a little person. Both of Becky's parents and older sister are "average" height, and her parents always taught her to stay positive no matter how harsh the outside world may be.

Becky says that she discovered the strength she needed to rise above challenges and learned that *true* disability could only be found in ones insecurities and the limitations we set for ourselves.

"We were all brought to this earth for a reason and have the ability to do whatever we want with our lives. The truth is that everyone struggles in their everyday life in one way or another. It's about staying positive and making the best of what you have."
— Becky Curran

Our real disabilities come from the inside. All of us, even those without any type of legally accepted

disability, can fall prey to self-defeating thinking by focusing on what we cannot do and comparing ourselves to others.

Here are Becky's tips for how to overcome any obstacle or perceived disability that life may put in front of you:

1. **Stay focused on the positives instead of the negatives.** No matter what obstacles have come my way, staying positive has allowed me to overcome them. When I was in tenth grade, I had to miss 29 days of school in order to have major back surgery, where seven vertebrae were removed due to spinal cord compression. I knew that the back surgery was crucial and I found a way to make up the school work that I had missed. Staying positive allowed me to keep up with my classmates and graduate on time.

2. **Don't ever give up.** When I first moved out to Los Angeles after growing up in Boston, I went on one hundred job interviews before starting my current position. If I wasn't right for those one hundred positions, I knew there still had to be an opportunity out there for me.

3. **Challenge yourself and try new things every day.** As soon as I wake up in the morning, I encounter a new challenge — whether it's trying to reach something high in the kitchen or volunteering to participate in an optional pitch lunch at work. As long as you try, that's all that matters in the end.

4. **Each day you should ask yourself if you're happy.** If there's something that's making you unhappy, you should find a way to make change. I find myself unhappy whenever I'm surrounded by negative people. Now I'm more cautious of the people with whom I surround myself.

5. **Smile.** A smile goes a long way. Whenever people are staring or laughing at me for whatever reason, keeping a smile on my face causes them to wonder why I don't react.

6. **Don't compare yourself to others and find time to celebrate your little accomplishments.** I always set my own goals. Although we all wish we could get there as fast as it seems others have, I've found ways to enjoy the journey and celebrate each little success on the way. After missing almost a whole season on the youth soccer team, due to my back surgery during the spring of my sophomore year in college, I found a way to play in the last game of the season. I never scored a goal but participating was just as important to me. After long recovery, this was a huge accomplishment for me" (Becky Curran).

"Next time you are out and about, try to find someone to smile at and say hello to. If they look like they're struggling, try to help them out. Take the chance to learn from them. Disability can only be found in the way you think and life is only as hard as you make it." — Becky Curran

There is no person born on the earth who will live an obstacle free life. Money will not grant you an obstacle free life. Faith in God will not grant you an obstacle free life. Fame will not give you an obstacle free life. No! We all face obstacles. *How*, we face them will determine the path that we take.

We can take the road of bitterness and end up on calamity avenue. Or we take the road of "count it all joy" and end up on peace avenue. Decide today to face your obstacles with dignity, integrity and authenticity.

The 8 Step Transformation Process will help you to get passed any obstacle that you are facing. Read on. The best is yet to come.

Key Points

When faced with a bump in the road, sometimes we forget we have a choice: overcome the obstacle or let it overcome you.

What bump are you currently facing on your road to success?

What are your choices?

Our real disabilities come from the inside. All of us, even those without any type of legally accepted disability, can fall prey to self-defeating thinking by focusing on what we cannot do and comparing ourselves to others.

What self-defeating thoughts have been handicapping you in your life's journey?

What can-not's have you been focusing on instead of the can-do's?

Who have you been comparing yourself to that is limiting you?

"Disability can only be found in the way you think and life is only as hard as you make it." - Becky Curran

What thoughts have you been having that is making your life harder than it needs to be?

Discovery Action Steps

Use Becky's tips to overcome any obstacle or perceived disability that life may put in front of you:

1. Stay focused on the positives instead of the negatives.
2. Don't ever give up.
3. Challenge yourself and try new things every day.
4. Each day you should ask yourself if you're happy.
5. Smile. A smile goes a long way.
6. Don't compare yourself to others and find time to celebrate your little accomplishments.

You can take the road of bitterness and end up on calamity avenue. Or you take the road of "count it all joy" and end up on peace avenue.

Will you decide today to face your obstacles with dignity, integrity, and authenticity?

CHAPTER 8
Alignment

There is a loving, beautiful, harmonious life awaiting you where you can live your life to its fullest. Being happy and having a healthy body, soul, and spirit is not only possible but attainable. It is the rule and not the exception. I am talking about a life where you experience joy deep down in your soul and where there is peace which you cannot describe. Joy unspeakable and full of glory! This full abundant life is available to anyone who is willing to seek after it.

Tapping into this life all depends on how bad you want it.

Make no mistake about it there are negative forces that will try to prevent you from getting to this point. These negative forces are everywhere and getting away from them is nearly impossible. You must make a concerted effort to rid your mind of negativity.

A number of years ago the National Science Foundation estimated that our brains produce as many as 12,000 to

50,000 thoughts per day depending on how deep a thinker you are (other estimates run as high as 60,000/day). Some people have estimated that upwards of 70-80 percent of our daily thoughts are negative. That is very sad if true. The human mind, it would seem, is wired for neuroticism.

A healthy first step to alleviate this problem, therefore, would be to increase one's awareness of these negative and bogus thoughts. This is what is referred to as mindfulness. It is a type of self-reflexivity and enhanced self-awareness that helps Buddhists root themselves in the moment. Once individuals have awareness of these thoughts they can sweep them away like fallen leaves.

Negativity is a disruptive, anxious vibration. Once your vibration becomes more peaceful, loving, and positive you position yourself to see your thoughts and reality become more obvious. As your thoughts become purer and less cluttered, you enter a dimension where you see the manifestation of your desires in the now.

Seek first the kingdom and everything else will come (see Matthew 6:33). The kingdom is attained through Jesus Christ and living the way that He lived and wants us to live. As you acknowledge His desires in your own life, you will discover the possibilities are endless. You will see that you will be able to accomplish goals and dreams that most only think about.

God is that light and in Him there is no darkness at all. There is no negativity. No jealousy, no hate, no fear and no bitterness—only love.

In order to walk in this vibration you need to be in complete alignment with the perfect frequency of Infinite Intelligence. There are four aspects that must be simultaneously accomplished:

- *Loving unconditionally*
- *Forgiving those who have hurt us*
- *Being obedient*
- *Living by faith*

Sound like a tall order? It is, but if you are willing to lay everything aside and go after it, you can do it. By these four conditions, you will find yourself in complete alignment to receive this abundant, positive life that I am speaking of.

Unconditional Love

Agape is selfless, sacrificial, unconditional love and is the highest of the four types of love spoken of in the Bible. This Greek word and variations of it are found throughout the New Testament. *Agape* perfectly describes the kind of love Jesus Christ has for His Father and for His followers.

> *Whoever has my commands and keeps them is the one who loves me. The one who loves me will be loved by my Father, and I too will love them and show myself to them.*
> *(John 14:21 NIV)*

This powerful emotion is the highest vibration and is critical in gaining access to the miracle zone. Tina

Turner asked, "What's love got to do with it?" The answer is *everything*. Without love you cannot freely give or receive anything from anyone. This is an area that I have had to work on. Accepting people with loving, open arms used to be a challenge for me. It was not until I learned how to love myself, flaws and all, that I was able to love others unconditionally. We are all imperfect beings who need love and acceptance. When I encounter someone who is hateful or vindictive or who is spewing out poison, I ask the question silently, "What happened to them or who hurt them?" Once you master this emotion you are on your way to creating a space where good can come to you in abundance.

Forgiveness

"To forgive is to set a prisoner free and discover that the prisoner was you," says Lewis B. Smedes.

"The weak can never forgive. Forgiveness is the attribute of the strong," said Mahatma Gandhi.

"Forgiveness is giving up the hope that the past could've been any different. So you don't hold on to wishing that you'd had a different kind of brother, a different kind of mother, a different kind of family. You let that go and you move forward with the grace that God has given you. From this day on, forgiveness is giving up the hope that the past could've been any different," shared Oprah Winfrey.

When someone you care about hurts you, you can hold on to anger, resentment, and thoughts of revenge—or embrace forgiveness and move forward.

"If you forgive yourself and atone and seek to do better now in the places where you've made mistakes, and if where other people have made mistakes that impacted you, are willing to stand in a space of forgiveness, then despite what anyone has done, including yourself that in any way led up to this moment of lack, the universe will miraculously and automatically create a new trajectory of probability, taking you back into a field of infinite abundance." - Marienne Williamsen

What motivates forgiveness? Often we view it as some kind of concession. We think we are being generous by granting it. However, in truth, *we* are the prime beneficiaries of forgiveness. When we forgive, we let go. When we forgive, we stop clinging to the pain. Continuing to be angry only makes things worse for us. Why would we devote so much energy to it? Bitterness does not make us feel better. Thus, forgiveness is in our own best interests.

When you feel forgiveness in your heart, it is easier to be happy, productive, accomplish your goals, and be at peace with yourself. Forgiving another is really less about other people and more about being true, kind, and respectful to ourselves. Likewise, humbly compensating for our transgressions against others is a way to give ourselves the esteem and value we deserve.

> **"Forgiveness is not an emotion... *Forgiveness is an act of the will, and the will can function regardless of the temperature of the heart.*"**
> — **Corrie Ten Boom**

Harboring hatred and not forgiving someone else can be detrimental to you. It can:

- *Rob you of your future and strip you of your destiny.*
- *Keep you trapped in bitterness, anger, and resentment.*
- *Make you feel hopeless, helpless, and hurt.*
- *Bring you physical or emotional pain.*
- *Make you sad and sour.*

Forgiveness has four levels. In order of walk in a place of hope, healing, and light it is important to apply forgiveness in each of these four levels.

Forgive Yourself

"Be gentle first with yourself if you wish to be gentle with others." - Lama Yeshe

Forgiving yourself may be the hardest of the four levels to accomplish. We have a tendency to be harder on ourselves than others are. Forgiving yourself can be much harder than forgiving someone else. The weight of carrying around past hurt, pain, and self-hatred is very dark and heavy. It is hard to experience joy, peace, and love while carrying around this negativity. Forgiving yourself is an important act of moving forward and releasing yourself from the past. It is also a way of protecting your health and general well-being.

Kwame Kilpatrick, former mayor of Detroit, was sentenced to twenty-eight years in prison. He was convicted of public corruption. At his sentencing he apologized to his family, friends, and to the citizens of Detroit. He said that he hoped that one day he could forgive himself.

You may have never committed a crime such as Kilpatrick, nevertheless there are unfortunate things that happened in life where we blame ourselves and often find it hard to receive forgiveness. You may have gone through a divorce or acted out in anger towards someone or perhaps you lied about someone and caused them to lose their job. No matter what you have done, forgiveness is available for you.

Remember these three things as you walk in forgiveness towards yourself:

1. *You are not a bad person. We all make mistakes.*
2. *Everyone has flaws and no one is perfect.*
3. *The sooner you do it the better you will feel.*

Ask God for Forgiveness

Let every soul be subject under the higher powers. For there is no power but of God: the powers that are ordained of God. We are all subject to authority and we put ourselves under a higher power. God has established a governing rule-His word, the Bible, and we must subject ourselves to His will.

Because I do not want to be out of the perfect will of God, I come under the authority of the Holy Spirit and yield to His commands. When I fail at doing this, my relationship with God becomes distant and I feel disconnected. I long to be in right relationship with Him again!

Asking God to forgive you can be a very humbling experience. Everyone has suffered some form of rejection or another, and the thought of being rejected by God is very scary. The thought of not receiving unconditional love and acceptance from God is unbearable.

There is a path laid out for you and me which leads to our destiny in life. We are on a journey and along that journey we miss opportunities, encounter pain, mess up, hurt people, get hurt, disappoint others and God. When we find ourselves bogged down with the cares of life it is important to analyze our situations and to let go of whatever is holding us down or hindering us. When we perceive that we are at fault, making it right is the only remedy to get us back on track.

Suppose you went out hiking one day somewhere in the mountains, and you brought along a very heavy backpack. The farther you hiked, the more exhausted you got, all because of that backpack. Then suppose someone came along who was obviously much stronger than you, and he offered to carry the backpack for you. What would you do? You could refuse, of course, perhaps out of pride or stubbornness. It would be far better for you to accept his offer and let him carry the backpack. Once you did, you would not be carrying it any longer. You would be free.

Think of the inability to forgive as the load in the backpack and the more you add to it the heavier it gets. When we ask God to forgive us, He takes the backpack and throws it away. Do not be afraid to ask God to forgive you. He will do it. You will feel like a burden has been lifted off of your shoulders.

Forgive Others

Forgiving those who have hurt us can be tough. "What motivates forgiveness? Often we view it as some kind of concession. We think we are being generous by granting it. However, in truth, we are the prime beneficiaries of forgiveness. When we forgive, we let go. When we forgive, we stop clinging to the pain. Continuing to be angry only makes things worse for us. Why would we devote so much energy to it? Bitterness does not make us feel better. Thus forgiveness is in our own best interests" (SpiritualInquiry.com).

I love this story. It was excerpted from "I'm Still Learning to Forgive" by Corrie ten Boom, and posted on the internet where it was reprinted by permission from *Guideposts* Magazine.

I love the part where she says, "Forgiveness is not an emotion… Forgiveness is an act of the will,

and the will can function regardless of the temperature of the heart."

The idea that you do not wait for the feeling, but start with the right action and hope the feeling will follow makes sense on so many levels. I will stop editorializing and let you read the whole story.

"It was in a church in Munich that I saw him—a balding, heavyset man in a gray overcoat, a brown felt hat clutched between his hands. People were filing out of the basement room where I had just spoken, moving along the rows of wooden chairs to the door at the rear. It was 1947 and I had come from Holland to defeated Germany with the message that God forgives.

"It was the truth they needed most to hear in that bitter, bombed-out land, and I gave them my favorite mental picture. Maybe because the sea is never far from a Hollander's mind, I liked to think that that's where forgiven sins were thrown. 'When we confess our sins,' I said, 'God casts them into the deepest ocean, gone forever.'

"The solemn faces stared back at me, not quite daring to believe. There were never questions after a talk in Germany in 1947. People stood up in silence, in silence collected their wraps, in silence left the room.

"And that's when I saw him, working his way forward against the others. One moment I saw the overcoat and the brown hat; the next, a blue uniform and a visored cap with its skull and crossbones. It came back with a rush:

the huge room with its harsh overhead lights; the pathetic pile of dresses and shoes in the center of the floor; the shame of walking naked past this man. I could see my sister's frail form ahead of me, ribs sharp beneath the parchment skin. *Betsie, how thin you were!* [Betsie and I had been arrested for concealing Jews in our home during the Nazi occupation of Holland; this man had been a guard at Ravensbruck concentration camp where we were sent.]

"Now he was in front of me, hand thrust out: 'A fine message, Fräulein! How good it is to know that, as you say, all our sins are at the bottom of the sea!'

"And I, who had spoken so glibly of forgiveness, fumbled in my pocketbook rather than take that hand. He would not remember me, of course—how could he remember one prisoner among those thousands of women?

"But I remembered him and the leather crop swinging from his belt. I was face-to-face with one of my captors and my blood seemed to freeze.

"'You mentioned Ravensbruck in your talk,' he was saying, 'I was a guard there.' No, he did not remember me.

"'But since that time,' he went on, 'I have become a Christian. I know that God has forgiven me for the cruel things I did there, but I would like to hear it from your lips as well. Fräulein,' again the hand came out—'will you forgive me?'

"And I stood there—I whose sins had again and again to be forgiven—and could not forgive. Betsie had died in that place—could he erase her slow terrible death simply for the asking?

"It could not have been many seconds that he stood there—hand held out—but to me it seemed hours as I wrestled with the most difficult thing I had ever had to do.

"For I had to do it—I knew that. The message that God forgives has a prior condition: that we forgive those who have injured us. 'If you do not forgive men their trespasses,' Jesus says, 'neither will your Father in heaven forgive your trespasses.'

"I knew it not only as a commandment of God, but as a daily experience. Since the end of the war I had had a home in Holland for victims of Nazi brutality. Those who were able to forgive their former enemies were able also to return to the outside world and rebuild their lives, no matter what the physical scars. Those who nursed their bitterness remained invalids. It was as simple and as horrible as that.

"And still I stood there with the coldness clutching my heart. But forgiveness is not an emotion—I knew that, too. Forgiveness is an act of the will, and the will can function regardless of the temperature of the heart. '... Help!' I prayed silently. 'I can lift my hand. I can do that much. You supply the feeling.'

"And so woodenly, mechanically, I thrust my hand into the one stretched out to me. And as I did, an incredible thing took place. The current started in my shoulder, raced down my arm, sprang into our joined hands. And then this healing warmth seemed to flood my whole being, bringing tears to my eyes.

"'I forgive you, brother!' I cried. 'With all my heart!

"For a long moment we grasped each other's hands, the former guard and the former prisoner. I had never known God's love so intensely, as I did then."[3]

Ask Others to Forgive You

One of the most overlooked aspects of forgiveness is how to ask for it. Asking for forgiveness should not be done according to human wisdom nor simply generated by emotional intensity. Asking for forgiveness should, instead, be based on biblical truth, especially with regard to personal responsibility and esteeming others as more important than one's self. Any important endeavor of life requires planning, and forgiveness is certainly one of those undertakings.

If you are a believer in Christ and ask another person to forgive you, be sure to speak the truth about your sin(s). Truth means "bringing everything to light." In the Bible, this is described as being verifiable, indisputable, without

---

[3] Excerpt from "I'm Still Learning to Forgive" by Corrie ten Boom. Reprinted by permission from Guideposts Magazine. Copyright © 1972 by Guideposts Associates, Inc., Carmel, New York 10512.

pretense or deception, devoid of any hint of falsehood, unconcealed, and complete with all the facts.

Asking for forgiveness can:

1. *Free, heal, nurture, and release you.*
2. *Fill you with light and love.*
3. *Ennoble, empower, and enlighten you.*
4. *Bring you closer to God.*
5. *Refresh, reward, and renew you.*

Obedience

The definition of obey is to comply with the command, direction, or request of (a person or a law); submit to authority (Google Dictionary). When you are seeking to transform your life you must be willing to do whatever you have been asked to do to insure success in whatever endeavor you are embarking upon. To transform means to change completely.

Disobedience can be very costly. Growing up being obedient was huge in our house. When momma and daddy asked you to do something you were expected to obey, and right now! Obedience was not a choice.

I must admit, though, that there is a part of me that wants to buck against the system. If the program says only eat certain things, I eat other things hoping to be able to gain the success that I would have gained if I had not veered off of the plan. I am the child who asked 100 questions before I would comply. I am the one who had a streak of disobedience in her and was always pushing the button. I remember when my dad allowed me to drive the car on a wintery, icy day in Michigan.

"Lynn", he said, "Stay on the main roads when you travel because the side streets are slipperier."

What does he know, I thought! Low and behold as I am traveling down one of the side streets I notice that the roads are very slippery. Even though I pumped my brakes, I could not stop and ran right into an oncoming car. Well, I learned my lesson that day and vowed to listen to and obey my dad from then on.

Faith

Without faith it is impossible to please God. Without believing that what He says is true will cause you to never be able to take hold of His promises of blessings. Anyone who wants to approach God must believe both that He exists *and* that He cares enough to respond to those who seek Him.

Today, more than ever it is so important that we walk by faith! There will never be a time in our lives that we will not need to exercise our faith, so we need to keep it strong!

Faith in God and putting our trust in His healing power can heal cancer and open blind eyes. Everything that you do requires a measure of faith even as small as a grain of mustard seed. God can only manifest His blessings in your life when you please Him. We please God through the faith and trust that we put in Him.

We are to trust God with all our hearts, and allow Him to manifest His best blessings in our lives. It is through faith that we can see the invisible, touch the intangible, and we can call things that be not as though they were. Simply put, we can see things manifest simply by speaking, believing, and not doubting in our heart.

> **And without faith it is impossible to please God, because anyone who comes to him must believe that he exists and that he rewards those who earnestly seek him.**
> **(Hebrews 11:6 NIV)**

Key Points

Tapping into this life all depends on how bad you want it.

God is that light and in Him there is no darkness at all. There is no negativity. No jealous, no hate, no fear and no bitterness—only love.

When someone you care about hurts you, you can hold on to anger, resentment and thoughts of revenge—or embrace forgiveness and move forward.

"Forgiveness is not an emotion… Forgiveness is an act of the will, and the will can function regardless of the temperature of the heart." - Corrie Ten Boom

"And without faith it is impossible to please God, because anyone who comes to him must believe that he exists and that he rewards those who earnestly seek him" (Hebrews 11:6 NIV).

Discovery Action Steps

Seek first the kingdom and everything else will come (see Matthew 6:33). The kingdom is attained through Jesus Christ and _____ the way that He _____ and wants us to_____.

In order to walk in and achieve the peace you seek, you need to be in complete alignment with the perfect frequency of Infinite Intelligence. There are four aspects that must be simultaneously accomplished. Define each one and then describe how you are going to implement it in your own life.

Loving unconditionally means _____

So I need to _____

Forgiveness means _____

So I need to _____

Being obedient means _____

So I need to _____

Living by faith means _____

So I need to _____

Forgiveness has four levels. In order of walk in a place of hope, healing and light it is important to apply forgiveness in each of these four levels. Begin today.

Forgive Yourself

Declare these three things as you walk in forgiveness towards yourself:

1. I am not a bad person. We all make mistakes including me.
2. Everyone has flaws and no one is perfect including me.
3. The sooner I do it the better I will feel.

Ask God for Forgiveness

Think of the inability to forgive as the load in the backpack and the more you add to it the heavier it gets. When you ask God to forgive you He takes the backpack and throws it away. Do not be afraid to ask God to forgive you. He will do it. You will feel like a burden has been lifted off of your shoulders.

Ask God to forgive you today.

Ask Others to Forgive You

If you are a believer in Christ and ask another person to forgive you, be sure to speak the truth about your sin(s). Truth means "bringing everything to light." In the Bible, this is described as being verifiable, indisputable, without pretense or deception, devoid of any hint of falsehood, unconcealed, and complete with all the facts.

> *Are you willing to bring everything to light and speak the truth?*

Obedience

The definition of obey is to comply with the command, direction, or request of (a person or a law); submit to authority.

> *Are you willing to do whatever you have been asked to do to insure success in whatever endeavor you are embarking upon?*

> *Will you trust God with all your heart, and allow Him to manifest His best blessings in your life today?*

CHAPTER 9
The Bucket List

"Every man dies – Not every man really lives." - William Ross

What is a Bucket List? It is a list of all the goals you want to achieve, dreams you want to fulfill, and life experiences you desire to experience before you die.

Ask yourself:

Is my life filled with mundane day to day activities?

Do I live my day with personal goals and plans?

Do I ever feel like life is passing me by without any tangible benefits?

What have I accomplished in the past three months?

What are my goals for the next three months?

Now look at the things you have done and the things you are planning to do next. Would they mean anything to you if you knew that you had a limited time to live?

Why Create a Bucket List?

Having a bucket list reminds you of what is really important so that you can act on them now. A bucket list offers you a no holds barred opportunity to do anything that you think would be fulfilling, exciting, and exhilarating. It is a forum to get anything and everything you have ever wanted to do, whether it is big, small or random.

A bucket list is about doing things that really matter and maximizing every moment of your existence.

It is just like planning ahead all the highlights you want for your whole life. The objective of creating this list is not to instill some kind of morbid thoughts about death and dying. Rather the idea is to begin to live your life with more meaning. It is about doing things that really matter and maximizing every moment of your existence.

Growing up in a small town of 3.6 square miles with a population of 10,000 people, I never really had much of a bucket list. Everyone knew everyone else. We were a very tight knit community. The biggest activity in town was going to Lottie's Candy Store, which was about two blocks from my house. Our lives revolved around home, church, and school. I do not remember being a dreamer or even having an active imagination as a child. I think I was just very real, too practical, and never had a check list of things that I wanted to do beyond the current day.

My husband, Michael, however, ran around the house with his sister and brothers making believe he was living in Africa as a child. The stories he tells me hint of how bright, vivid, and healthy his imagination was as child.

The Power of Fear

Fear is a terrible thing. Fear will rob you of your imagination and innocence. Fear will rob you of your dreams. It will blind you to what you can become. It will smother you. I think fear tried to rob me of my bucket list. Fear was with me as a child and stayed with me on into my young adult life. As I grew older fear turned into intimidation and insecurity.

Even with these challenges I was able to make some significant accomplishments including going to college. I ended up a student at Western Michigan University. I really do not know how I ended up there, but it was the beginning of a different life for me.

As a student in college I began to make a concerted effort to better myself. I began to ask myself some very serious questions. Where was I going? What was I going to do with my life? What was I going to be? All of these thoughts rolled around in my head like a fish swimming around in a small round fish bowl. I knew that I had decisions to make. If I was ever going to be able to identify who I was, where I was going, and what I wanted to do with my life, I had to come clean and get rid of the baggage I was carrying.

Dealing with the demons of intimidation, fear, and insecurity was no longer an option! Dreams, thoughts and ideas of living a fun, exciting and adventurous life were trying to emerge, but I knew that I would never be able to live my dreams without addressing my issues. How I would rid myself of these demons was something that I had not figured out yet, but I knew I wanted more out of life than what I was living.

The Answer

I had no idea how my deliverance would come and was thoroughly surprised when it came in the form of a man. One afternoon I saw him at the student union of the college we both attended, Western Michigan University. The man who would become my husband was tall, Mocha brown, and handsome. He was bubbly, witty, full of life, and most of all fearless. He knew how to live life to the fullest.

It was the fall of 1978 and he was on his way to Washington, D.C. with a bunch of other students he did not know, to protest the reign of the Shah of Iran. He could have cared less about the cause. All he wanted was a free trip to Washington, D. C. because it was a place he had never visited. *Who is this man*, I thought, *who would do something so crazy and adventurous?* Something inside of me admired his courage and passion for life. At that moment I wanted to throw caution to the wind and experience what he was experiencing. He was free and I longed for that freedom.

We all come with an expiration date attached to our lives. There is appointed to man a time to be born and a time to die. In between that space is a time to live. It is the "dash" between the dates on our tombstones. What we do with that time is up to each of us. It is when we live out our bucket list.

When Michael came into my life, he was on my bucket list or I should say that getting married to a wonderful man kind of like my dad was on my list. Having him in my life made me want to dream bigger and to reach higher. He made me want to deal with the demons of fear, intimidation, and insecurity because I wanted to experience this freedom that he exhibited.

We began to create our bucket list, individually and collectively:

Get married, check.

Visit Africa, check.

Have children, check.

Serve God, check.

Build a strong family unit, check.

Do missions work, check.

Grow a church, check.

Build a house, check.

Stay at a five-star hotel, check.

Do philanthropic work, check.

We were well on our way to living an abundant life. One of the items on Michael's bucket list was to travel to Israel. As a young man in college the Holy Spirit spoke to him and told him that he would be connecting with the Jewish people and that he would one day travel to Israel. It was uncanny how his relationship with a Jewish man who owned a dry cleaning business lead to another relationship with another Jewish man, Elisha Ben-yitzak, owner of Heavenly International Tours. From that introduction we began leading tours to Israel and have, to date, collectively traveled to the Holy Land, nine times.

Did you ever get a chance to see the movie "The Bucket List"? The story revolves around corporate billionaire, Edward Cole (Jack Nicholson) and working class mechanic, Carter Chambers (Morgan Freeman) who have nothing in common except for their terminal illnesses. While sharing a hospital room together, they decide to leave and do all the things they ever wanted to do on their bucket lists before they died. In the process, they become unlikely friends and ultimately find joy in life in spite of their terminal illness diagnosis.

What will it take to make you start to do things on your bucket list? Do not wait until tragedy strikes or until you get to a certain age. Start filling in the space between the "dash" now. If you do not have a bucket list, create one and start living large and in color.

Different Types of Bucket Lists

Elizabeth Scott wrote an article titled, "How to Create a Bucket List," in an online blog titled, "About Health."[4] In it she described different kinds of bucket lists. It may be helpful for you to review these and see if one helps you start your own bucket.

Traditional: The traditional bucket list is a list of things you would like to do before you die.

Birthday: It is also inspiring to create a bucket list of what you hope to experience and accomplish in the coming year before your next birthday.

Milestone: If you would like to make the most of your experiences, you can create a bucket list for each phase of life. For example, a College Bucket List can help you to make the most of your college years and ensure you get closer to meeting all of your goals and expectations for that period of your life. There are Summer Bucket Lists, Pregnancy Bucket Lists, a bucket list for your kids' childhood experiences, and bucket lists for other phases of life.

Goals: Maintaining a Goal's Bucket List can help you to get in touch with what you feel is important for your life overall in terms of achievement. List what you would like

---

[4] We need a complete reference here. http://stress.about.com/od/resolutionsandchanges/a/How-To-Create-A-Bucket-List.htm

to accomplish in five years, ten years, and twenty years and see where you can go from there.

Here are some of the bucket list ideas that I found on the Internet on various sites:

A girl writes that she wants to see a sunrise in Italy, meet and fall in love with a great guy, and become a successful writer.

A young man says that he wants to be a race car driver, travel the world, and climb Mount Kilimanjaro.

Finally a mother dreams of seeing all eleven of her children graduate from college.

Dr. Myles Munroe

I sat spellbound on Facebook watching news emerge about whether Dr. Myles Munroe and his wife were among the nine people killed aboard a small Bahamas-bound aircraft that crashed. The internationally known motivational speaker had been on his way to the Global Leadership Forum hosted by the Bahamas Faith Ministries, an organization Munroe founded. As time passed, it was confirmed that Dr. Myles Munroe and his beautiful wife Ruth were among the nine people killed in that aircraft crash.

Dr. Munroe was an internationally renowned, bestselling author, lecturer, teacher, life coach, government consultant, and leadership mentor. He travelled around the world training leaders in business, government, education, sports, media, and religion. He was known for his teaching on the subjects of "purpose and "potential." He leaves a tremendous legacy in books and training materials about living life on purpose and making every day count.

Dr. Munroe lived life to its fullest. He valued every moment and encouraged us to do the same. One of his famous quotes is, "The greatest tragedy in life is not death, but life without a purpose."

Getting In Touch With Your Values

When you make a list of all the things you would like to do, this activity may be a springboard to becoming more aware of what is really important to you. When you start thinking about what you really want to do, you can find perspective on how you are currently spending your time, and on what you would like to be doing. This will give you the time and energy for things that really matter to you. Making a bucket list can help you remember what you value the most and eliminate the things that really do not matter, but eat up your time and energy.

> Your bucket list should contain the deep desires of your heart.

Key Points

A bucket list is about doing things that really matter and maximizing every moment of your existence.

A bucket list is a springboard to becoming more aware of what is really important to you.

Your bucket list should contain the deep desires of your heart.

Discovery Action Steps

Ask Yourself:

What are some of the things I would like to do or places I would like to visit before I kick the bucket?

What are the dreams that I have yet to see fulfilled?

What is in my heart to do that I have not done?

How do you make a bucket list?

- Get out your notepad and find a comfortable spot to think and dream.
- Start by thinking about the things that are important to you.
- Write those things down.
- Do some research and brainstorm for creative ways to fulfill the ideas that come to mind. It may start as a raw thought. For example, your dream is to go on a family road trip during Spring break.
- Solidify the idea by researching possible ways to fulfill that first item on your list. In the example above you can start by googling locations and destinations which are not over seven or eight hours driving time away from your home.

- Then make a selection based on budget and other criteria that you establish.

Continue with this exercise by filling in the blank with everything you have ever hoped to do:

One day I hope to _____

To qualify for the list, it must be something that really matters to you. There may be things on your list that others will laugh at so only share with people who will not discourage you from pursuing your bucket list. Do not be shy. Whatever it is, you will feel fantastic crossing them off of your list one by one.

Here is a list of other bucket list ideas to get you started:

- Sail the Greek Islands
- Surf in Rapa Nui
- Meet Chuck Norris
- See Holland in bloom
- Meet President Obama
- Run a marathon
- Visit Ireland
- Watch a sunset in the Bahamas
- Go snorkeling off the Florida coast
- Visit Africa
- Have a wild deer eat out of your hand

CHAPTER 10
I Am a Witness

Your job is to speak out on the things that make for solid doctrine. Guide older men into lives of temperance, dignity, and wisdom, into healthy faith, love, and endurance. Guide older women into lives of reverence so they end up as neither gossips nor drunks, but models of goodness. By looking at them, the younger women will know how to love their husbands and children, be virtuous and pure, keep a good house, be good wives. We don't want anyone looking down on God's Message because of their behavior. Also, guide the young men to live disciplined lives. But mostly, show them all this by doing it yourself, incorruptible in your teaching, your words solid and sane. Then anyone who is dead set against us, when he finds nothing weird or misguided, might eventually come around. **(Titus 2:6-8 MSG)**

I am a witness to the power of belief in God and the Eight-step Transformation Process. These eight steps to miracles have proven themselves to work for everyone who has applied them. They will work for you as they have for others because the equipment God gave others is no different than yours.

> **God has given you everything you need for a life of abundance, prosperity, and peace. You are an overcomer and equipped to accomplish the dream and vision He has placed within you. If all of these people can achieve it so can you!**

Time and time again I have witnessed what making positive changes in one's life can do. Making a complete turnaround from a life filled with negativity to a life filled with abundance, prosperity, and peace is possible when you apply these eight steps.

The Eight-step Transformation Process:

- Step One: Know The Truth
- Step Two: Transform Your Mind
- Step Three: Determine What You Really Want
- Step Four: Activate Your New Life
- Step Five: Be Open-Minded
- Step Six: Give
- Step Seven: Be All In
- Step Eight: Walk in New Beginnings

Any person who has ever achieved greatness of any magnitude has to have a strategy, a plan in place, and be willing to go through a process. These true stories will give you just a few varied examples of God's power at work, and show you what is possible when you are willing to go through the eight steps that are contained in this book.

Reading these true life stories will be extremely beneficial and will build your faith as you get a glimpse of the possibilities for you and others who may be in need. All you need to do is apply the teachings in the next few chapters and believe you can do it, too. I am sharing these stories of hope, fulfilling dreams, and achieving vision to encourage and inspire you to keep on dreaming and to build your faith. I will introduce you to the Eight-step Transformation Process in the next chapter and give you practical ways to apply these steps in your own life. First begin to build your faith as you read these true stories of people just like you who have overcome through igniting the strength within through the power of faith in God's love and promises.

> *You've all been to the stadium and seen the athletes race. Everyone runs; one wins. Run to win. All good athletes train hard. They do it for a gold medal that tarnishes and fades. You're after one that's gold eternally. I don't know about you, but I'm running hard for the finish line. I'm giving it everything I've got. No sloppy living for me! I'm staying alert and in top condition. I'm not going to get caught napping, telling everyone else all about it and then missing out myself.*
> *(1 Corinthians 9:24-27 MSG)*

My Husband: From Dream to Reality

My husband is a storyteller by nature. He tells the best stories ever. One of my favorite stories is about when he was growing up in Adrian, Michigan. My husband, his two brothers, Ralph, Robert, and their sister Inez would make sugar and butter sandwiches and toasted them on the heat register. After eating their sandwiches, they would start singing and running around the house calling each other the African names that they had given each other. They believed as children that they were going to Africa. From a very young age Michael knew that he would one day travel to Africa. He did not just dream, he did his part and put action to his vision. He has traveled to Africa more than once.

> **If my husband could overcome poverty and fulfill his dream so can you!**

From Grief to a Master's Degree in Business Administration

Another story comes to mind of a mother who was a member of our church in Milwaukee, Wisconsin. When her son committed suicide she knew that getting through this tragedy would be difficult. She also knew she could not allow her grief to paralyze her. Through prayer and applying the eight-step transformation process she not only got through it, but returned to school and received her Bachelor's Degree. Then she went on to receive her Master's Degree in Business Administration. Today she serves on staff at a non-profit organization as an accountant. She chose to take a tragic situation and allow it to propel her to achieving the potential within her.

If this mother can overcome her grief and become productive with her life so can you!

Swimmer Diana Nyad Finds a Way

I was privileged to hear this story of long distance swimmer and journalist Diana Nyad. As I listened to this powerful motivational speaker and author tell how she swam the 110-mile passage from Cuba to Florida, I thought if she can doing something like that, we can surely find a way to fulfill our dreams and visions. Nyad, a sixty-four-year-old woman, defied all the odds and through faith, perseverance, and belief accomplished her goal. The fifty-three hour swim was grueling, to say the least, and left her body bruised, bitten, and bloated. She managed to avoid drowning or being eaten by sharks. Nyad became the first person to swim from Cuba to Florida without the help of a shark cage.

Nyad had attempted this swim four previous times. She could have given up, but on her fifth attempt she was determined that this time she would make it.

Shortly after landing in Florida, she said: "I have three messages for you:

One is we should never, ever give up.

Two is you are never too old to chase your dreams.

Three endurance swimming looks like a solitary sport, but it takes a team."

"Find a way," she said to one interviewer.

Diana Nyad certainly proved that where there is a will there is a way.

If a sixty-four-year-old woman who failed the first four times can find a way and beat the odds, so can you!

A Tremendous Man of Faith

Lee Causey is a tremendous man of faith whose life mission was birthed out of the pain of seeing his brother who was born with polio, unable to walk. Lee became his brother's arms and legs, carrying him on his shoulders.

Lee was stirred at a deep emotional level to do something for people like his brother. This set him on his journey. After earning a football scholarship to the University of Florida, Lee soon realized his interest was the pursuit of creating and maintaining health and wellness through nutrition and exercise rather than through surgery.

In the early 1960s, Lee began to lay the groundwork for the first ever "diet shake," a product which today is manufactured by hundreds of companies, and responsible for generating billions of dollars in sales worldwide.

Before long, Lee became known as a wellness expert to many celebrities, athletes, and notable leaders. In the

70s, he broke new ground with the creation of his first nutritional company "Slender Now," which was touted by the Wall Street Journal as the fastest growing privately held company in history. He has since created more than 300 nutritional and weight loss products. He founded First Fitness Nutrition in 1989.

On numerous occasions I have had the pleasure of listening to Mr. Causey, even having been invited to his home. He is a mentor among mentors and has dedicated his life to empowering others. It is because of Lee's faith, belief, love of people, diligence, and perseverance that thousands of lives have been made better financially, physically, and mentally.

> **Lee Causey saw a need and pursued a way to do something about it. If he can do it so can you!**

Joe L. Dudley, Sr.

Michael and I had the opportunity to spend the day with Joe L. Dudley, Sr., President and Chief Executive Officer (CEO) of Dudley Products, Inc. His company is one of the world's largest manufacturers and distributors of hair care and beauty products. Born May 9, 1937, he is the fifth of eleven children born to Gilmer L. and Clara Yeates Dudley. Joe grew up in a three-room farm house in the rural community of Aurora, in eastern North Carolina.

Joe failed the first grade. He was labeled mentally retarded, and suffered a speech impediment. His mother never stopped believing in him and is responsible for encouraging him to overcome these obstacles and become a role model for many others living with physical handicaps.

Today, all around the world he is a well-respected entrepreneur and humanitarian. The hair care industry is a billionaire industry and Mr. Dudley is responsible for playing a huge part in its growth and development.

Throughout our time together Mr. Dudley shared his excitement about further opportunities that he foresaw. He offers these words of wisdom to people everywhere who need encouragement to achieve their dreams.

1. Never give up on your dreams.
2. Use what others see as your challenge to your advantage.
3. If you can believe it you can achieve.

If a man who failed the first grade, was labeled mentally retarded, and suffered a speech impediment can overcome these obstacles and become a role model for many others living with physical handicaps so can you!

After reading these inspirational stories I am sure that you cannot wait to learn how to apply the Eight-step Transformation Process to your own life. The fact that there are eight steps is no coincidence. The number eight is the number of new beginnings. You can start fresh today and achieve the dreams that you have only thought you could achieve. Let today be a fresh start for you. I am excited to help you get started on this exciting journey. I hope you are, too.

Key Points

God has given you everything you need for a life of abundance, prosperity, and peace. You are an overcomer and equipped to accomplish the dream and vision He has placed within you. If all of these people can achieve it so can you!

If my husband could overcome poverty and fulfill his dream so can you!

If a sixty-four-year-old woman who failed the first four times can find a way and beat the odds, so can you!

Lee Causey saw a need and pursued a way to do something about it. If he can do it so can you!

If a man who failed the first grade, was labeled mentally retarded, and suffered a speech impediment can overcome these obstacles and become a role model for many others living with physical handicaps so can you!

Discovery Action Steps

1. Never, ever give up on your dreams.
2. Use what others see as your challenge to your advantage.
3. If you can believe it you can achieve.

4. You are never too old to chase your dreams.
5. Look for needs and discover ways to do something about them.

Why not make 1 Corinthians 9:24-27 your declaration today:

You've all been to the stadium and seen the athletes race. Everyone runs; one wins. Run to win. All good athletes train hard. They do it for a gold medal that tarnishes and fades. You're after one that's gold eternally. I don't know about you, but I'm running hard for the finish line. I'm giving it everything I've got. No sloppy living for me! I'm staying alert and in top condition. I'm not going to get caught napping, telling everyone else all about it and then missing out myself. (1 Corinthians 9:24-27 MSG)

CHAPTER 11
The Eight-Step Transformation Process Part 1

The Eight-step Transformation Process:
- Step One: Know The Truth
- Step Two: Transform Your Mind
- Step Three: Determine What You Really Want
- Step Four: Activate Your New Life
- Step Five: Be Open-Minded
- Step Six: Give
- Step Seven: Be All In
- Step Eight: Walk in New Beginnings

The Eight-step Transformation Process (8STP) is a spiritual system designed to be completed in a sequential process, which when followed properly will give you tremendous blessings beyond belief. You will be renewed spirit, soul, and body. The number eight is associated with new beginnings, resurrection, and regeneration. When you go through the **8STP** you will experience change and transition from the old life into a new life filled with abundance, light, love, and peace. New beginnings are yours today.

Although I have followed this process for many years, it was after reading Kay Haugen's book, *From the Poorhouse to the Penthouse*, that I was I inspired to develop my own system and to teach it to others. There are countless thousands of people who are living the life of their dreams by applying the principles of this eight-step process and many thousands upon thousands who will use the **8STP** to see their lives transformed into the life that they have always dreamed of.

Each of the eight steps is important and must be completed in the order that they were created. It is very important to not put the cart before the horse, as it were. Following the **8STP** exactly as it is designed will open the door to a wellspring of undiscovered potential. There is a method to how the system is put together. Each step is necessary for advancement and must be completed in concert with the other steps. Missing or skipping a step will not give you the desired results.

In order to achieve the highest level of success with this program there must be total commitment from you. What you put in you will get out. You will reap exactly what you sow. I urge you to follow the program to the greatest extent that you can.

Your life is what it is today because of the thoughts and actions that you have taken. Your life is the manifestation of your belief system. If you are completely satisfied with where you are in life, what you have achieved and attained, and do not want anything more, you may not need to continue reading. However, if you know that there is more for you in this life, continue on with the **8STP** and you will begin to experience the most amazing life.

If you are committed to seeing change in your life, then you are in for a radical transformation.

Step One: Know the Truth

And you shall know the truth, and the truth shall make you free. (John 8:32)

God created the world and therefore He owns it and has authority and dominion over everything (Psalm 24:1). God set up His Kingdom in the Garden of Eden, placed Adam and Eve there, and gave them dominion to rule the earth. It was there that they received instructions from God and were commanded to go forth and rule with their God given dominion (Genesis 1:28).

Man and woman are not just to live on earth without reason, responsibility, or purpose. Their right to rule over God's creation is linked to them being made in the image of God for a certain purpose. Adam and Eve became the delegated authority over all creation.

God's Natural Laws

There are three schools of natural law theory: *divine natural law, secular natural law, and historical natural law.*

Divine natural law represents the system of principles believed to have been revealed or inspired by God or some other supreme and supernatural being. These divine principles are typically reflected by authoritative religious writings such as Scripture.

Secular natural law represents the system of principles derived from the physical, biological, and behavioral laws of nature as perceived by the human intellect and elaborated through reason.

Historical natural law represents the system of principles that has evolved over time through the slow accretion of custom, tradition, and experience.

Each school of natural law influenced the Founding Fathers during the nascent years of U.S. law in the eighteenth century and continue to influence the decision making process of state and federal courts today.[5]

Mel Thompson says, "Natural Law is of the most influential moral theories of all time–still a key feature of Catholic morality. It is also important because it links morality with belief in God-a direct bridge between ethics and the philosophy of religion."

---

5 Freedictionary http://legal-dictionary.thefreedictionary.com/Natural+Law

If you believe in a rational, creating, and designing God then you are likely to find Natural Law a convincing approach. If you find Natural Law convincing, then you are likely to be attracted to some idea of belief in God, or at least belief in the world as a designed and ordered place.

The Natural Law theory originated in Aristotle's idea that everything has a purpose that is revealed in its design, and that its supreme good is to be sought in fulfilling that purpose. Natural laws exist because the universe has a Creator God who is logical and has imposed order on His universe. Hence God created man with a divine purpose in mind.

Natural and a Supernatural God

We are spirit and are co-creators with God. We have been given access to vast amount of possibilities and power. To unlock this power requires us to understand our purpose here on earth. To have been created by God and given authority to rule and to tap into these unlimited resources is something that no other creature on earth can claim. We have unlimited access to God's infinite power, but there is a problem. In order to realize our full potential we have to believe it! We have to understand that limits are self-imposed.

Our purpose in this life is to co-create with God and help others to fulfill their potential in the earth. We were created without limitations. God our Father created us to do His bidding in the earth, experience His miraculous healing power, and to usher mankind back to Him. Our role model is God-incarnate, Jesus Christ, who operates without limitations. His very birth is the greatest miracle to have ever taken place in the history of mankind.

> **You are pregnant with promise, potential, and possibilities. Miracles only happen to and for those who believe.**

God is spirit (a spiritual being) and those who worship Him must worship Him in spirit and in truth (reality). Humans are made in the image of God and are therefore spiritual beings as well. The only way to communicate with God is spirit to spirit. The only way to worship God is through our spirit.

Intuition

Have you ever sensed that something was going to happen? Or saw something in your mind's eye that would later actually happen? Or perhaps you heard a word or phrase that was a precursor for an event or incident that occurred?

In her book *Divine Guidance*, Doreen Virtue explains that we have constant access to divine guidance from God and the angels. We could say that God and angels speak to us through our intuition. Doreen writes, "God and the angels have always spoken to you continuously. They have been guiding, coaxing, and encouraging you since you were first created."

It has been said that intuition is a direct link to our soul, our highest self, God or the universal mind. Intuition is often referred to as our sixth sense.

The truth is that human beings are spiritual beings connected to other human beings through the spiritual realm. We are powerful beyond our imagination.

Practice the truth and the truth will make you free. Hearing the truth is fascinating. Knowing the truth is liberating! Speaking the truth is invigorating!

New Truths Are Shaped By What You Say About Yourself.

Changing your mind and the words that you speak about yourself is a process. You have to intentionally think about what you are thinking about, and you have to intentionally say positive things to and about yourself.

Affirmations really are simple. They are you being in conscious control of your thoughts. They are short, powerful, positive statements. When you say them or think them or even hear them, they become the thoughts that create your reality. Affirmations, then, are your conscious thoughts.

When speaking affirmations it is important to speak them with emotion. We have feelings and getting our whole person involved will help to seal our affirmations in our heart and mind quicker.

In my past life I did not understood who I was or what my purpose was, but today I walk in the truth and have stepped into who I am supposed to be. I submit myself to the process of change so that I may embrace the new possibilities that await me. I have no doubt or fear and accept truth in my inward parts. I am discovering who I am more each day.

Begin by speaking these truths:

I am set free by the truth.

Nothing is impossible.

I have unlimited possibility.

What I believe, God's power can effortlessly achieve.

I let go of all negativity and embrace the truth.

Step Two: Transform Your Mind

Do not be conformed to this world (this age), [fashioned after and adapted to its external, superficial customs], but be transformed (changed) by the [entire] renewal of your mind [by its new ideals and its new attitude], so that you may prove [for yourselves] what is the good and acceptable and perfect will of God, even the thing which is good and acceptable and perfect [in His sight for you].
(Romans 12:2 AMP)

Have you ever taken the time to think about what you are thinking about? Have you ever caught yourself thinking negative or destructive thoughts and redirected your thoughts? What do you spend time thinking about all day? Are your thoughts positive or negative? Are they happy or sad, encouraging or discouraging? Are they filled with life or filled with death? At a recent funeral of a lovely young woman, it was revealed that she had spent the last eight years planning her funeral. The doctors told her eight years ago that she was going to die. She spent many waking moments planning her funeral and thinking about death. That is no way for anyone to live.

Our thoughts lead to our actions. The battle is in the mind. What we think about today becomes our reality tomorrow.

We must spend our time thinking thoughts that are good, pure, lovely, honest and of integrity. What we think we become.

Cynthia's Story

Cynthia was raised in a large family by her mother and father. Her parent's relationship was less than ideal and the children felt the lack of true, genuine, love, and concern that was missing from their relationship. Cynthia, feeling a void in her life, became promiscuous and went from one boyfriend to the other. Upon finding the one man that she felt really loved and valued her, she had three children by him. As she grew older she realized that the relationship was not going anywhere so she decided to leave him and take her children. When she left she only had a high school diploma. Through the process of listening to messages shared in our church, receiving encouraging words, and changing her thinking today she has an MBA from a very prominent university.

I challenge you today to begin a renovation of your mind. Tear down the old dilapidated frame and structure and start building with a fresh, new foundation that can hold the new life prints you are creating.

> **"The aphorism, 'As a man thinketh in his heart so is he,' not only embraces the whole of a man's being, but is so comprehensive as to reach out to every condition and circumstance of his life. A man is literally what he thinks, his character being the complete sum of all his thoughts." - James Allen, As A Man Thinketh**

How do you transform your mind? Transforming your mind is a process. You have to renew your mind and change what you put into it by consistently meditating on good and positive thoughts.

Get Rid of All Negativity

We think over 40,000 thoughts a day and many of those thoughts are negative. If we are not paying attention to what we are thinking, chances are we are thinking unproductive and things. It is so important to fill your mind with good, positive thoughts.

Empty yourself of negative thoughts. Are you a conduit of blessing or a log filled dam of negativity?

God's creative power is like a perfect, pure, bright, white light which shines through our individualized consciousness. If we provide a clear conduit for it to travel through, supernatural possibilities beyond our previously conceived ideas of possibility will become easily available to us.

Low Grade Emotions

Negativity is dark and is a low grade emotion which takes your energy and your creativity. It clogs up the rivers of life, health, and healing. You need to allow the light of God to penetrate those dark negative places.

Here are some of the low grade emotions and actions that you must deal with and rid yourself of:

Adultery

Fornication

Uncleanness

Lasciviousness

Idolatry

Witchcraft

Hatred

Variance or Inconsistency

Emulations or Imitations

Wrath and Anger

Strife

Seditions and Subversions

Heresies

Envying

Murder

Drunkenness

Reveling

When you engage in these types of thoughts, behaviors, and emotions you deny yourself access to the many supernatural possibilities that are yours for the asking.

As God's perfect, raw creative light shines through you, it can be either impeded or highly accelerated into the present state of your individualized consciousness. The lower emotions of darkness that exist within the field of your consciousness can radically slow God's creative process. It can affect your "belief-to-reality" time frame in an extremely negative way by taking goals that could have happened instantaneously and drawing their accomplishment out over inordinately long periods of time, even years.

However, a clear conscience makes instantaneous results possible.

The goal of step two is to align yourself so perfectly with the frequency of God that the results that you are looking for happen almost instantaneously. The portals of heaven will open up for you and you will advance by leaps and bounds. You will experience radically quick results. Experiencing quick or immediate results will build your faith concerning your newfound belief system. "Now faith" is activated in your life!

In the beginning God created the heavens and the earth. When God said "let there be light," there *was* light. There was no delay in seeing the manifestation of what He spoke. This is the place that you must get to as well.

There is a divine order and a way to align yourself so that you begin to see immediate manifestations of prayers prayed through Jesus Christ. Everyone has a right to his or her own religious beliefs. I align myself with Christianity and the teachings of the Bible. Each person has been given a measure of faith whereby he can access God.

All people, be they Buddhist, Hindu, Muslim, Agnostic and Atheist can achieve a limited degree of access to the God source within through righteous, clean, and disciplined living.

However, the truth that will set Men free is that the only person to have ascended to the perfect frequency of spiritual authority is God, the one creator of all of mankind and the creator of the Universe. He is a triune being: God the Father, God the Son, and God the Holy Spirit. Each person of the trinity has a specific assignment.

Jesus said to him, I am the Way and the Truth and the Life; no one comes to the Father except by (through) Me. (John 14:6 AMP)

Flesh or Spirit

Man is also a triune being comprised of spirit, soul (the seat of your emotions) and body, the physical part. Man is a spirit who lives in a body and has a soul.

> *"The body is the house of the soul, and the soul is the house of the spirit."* - Justin Martyr[6]

> *"Spirit is all in all, and is not subject to imperfection or disease; Soul, the inter-medial reservoir of psychical potencies, is subject to ethers, fluids, foods, time, space, motion, temperature, temptation, disorder, disease, and the change termed death; the body, the outermost material garment, evolved from the soul elements, is subject by induction to each and every condition and alteration which is natural to and inseparable from the soul – in this rudimental sphere."* --Andrew Jackson Davis

My position is that the spirit of man remains perfect. The body is the house of the soul and the soul is the house of the spirit. When the body dies, the soul, having been subject to all that the body has experienced, may on first entering into the realms of spirit, be in need of recovery, but that vehicle or the soul is not the spirit. It is its form of manifestation in both the physical and the spiritual realm. Eventually, as the spirit evolves in understanding and achieves by the experiences of existing through the soul and the physical body, will overrule the soul and physical and be manifested as "pure spirit, pure light."

The threefold nature of man might be illustrated in several ways. Dr. Clarence Larkin uses three circles. The

---

6. http://www.spiritualismlink.com/ Justin Martyr, p. 210

outer circle stands for the *body* of man, the middle circle for the *soul,* and the inner for the *spirit.*

"In the outer circle the Body is shown as touching the Material world through the five senses of Sight, Smell, Hearing, Taste and Touch. The Gates to the Soul are Imagination, Conscience, Memory, Reason and the Affections. The Spirit receives impressions of outward and material things through the soul. The spiritual faculties of the Spirit are Faith, Hope, Reverence, Prayer and Worship." (Dr. Clarence Larkin, Rightly Dividing the Word, page 86).

The Holy Spirit

In this day we are experiencing the interworking of the Holy Spirit in our lives in a great manner. Do you have the Holy Spirit advantage working on your behalf? Do you know that the Holy Spirit has gifts and blessings that He wants to impart to you? The Holy Spirit is the doorway to the supernatural realm of possibility that exists right here, right now. The Holy Spirit will also lead you down the path of light that has been set for you. Many people do not ask the Holy Spirit to lead and to direct them. They leave the Holy Spirit out of the equation thereby leaving them confused, left wanting, and never quite obtaining all that is available for them.

For those who are interested in acquiring the consciousness of the Holy Spirit who is the perfect conduit for the supernatural power of God to flow through them, according to the Bible it begins with baptism. To achieve

Christ's promise of a limitless supply and supernatural possibilities, there are several required steps for higher levels of alignment you will need to take that only Jesus our beloved master has given us.

The first step is to do the cleansing exercise given in the action step portion of this chapter.

Key Points

If you are committed to seeing change in your life, then you are in for a radical transformation.

You are pregnant with promise, potential, and possibilities. Miracles only happen to and for those who believe.

Practice the truth and the truth will make you free. Hearing the truth is fascinating. Knowing the truth is liberating! Speaking the truth is invigorating!

Our thoughts lead to our actions. The battle is in the mind. What we think about today becomes our reality tomorrow.

"The aphorism, 'As a man thinketh in his heart so is he,' not only embraces the whole of a man's being, but is so comprehensive as to reach out to every condition and circumstance of his life. A man is literally what he thinks, his character being the complete sum of all his thoughts" (James Allen, As A Man Thinketh).

However, a clear conscience makes instantaneous results possible.

Discovery Action Steps

Here are some of the low grade emotions and actions that you must deal with and rid yourself of. Cross them off as you deal with them and eliminate them from your thinking.

Adultery

Fornication

Uncleanness

Lasciviousness

Idolatry

Witchcraft

Hatred

Variance or Inconsistency

Emulations or Imitations

Wrath and Anger

Strife

Seditions and Subversions

Heresies

Envying

Murder

Drunkenness

Reveling

Cleansing Exercise: This exercise is dedicated to helping you get the things out of your life that will hinder and block your blessings! It is also designed to open up the portals whereby the blessings can flow. The length of time it takes to get through this process is dependent upon how much you have to get rid of.

For this exercise you need to make this a series of lists:

    Bad Habits List

    Asking Others for Forgiveness List

    Forgiving Yourself List

    Forgiving Others List

    Asking God for Forgiveness List

    Character Flaws List

    House Cleaning Projects List

    Get Your House in Order List

    Jealousy List

    Greed List

    Excuses List

    Lack of Accepting Responsibility for Your Life List (Your Blame Game List)

    Disobedience List

    Your Associations List

    Teaching that Is Contrary to God's Word List

CHAPTER 12
The Eight-Step Transformation Process Part 2

Step Three: Determine What You Really Want

If you want to live an extraordinary life it is imperative that you *explore and learn* who you truly are. When you find this out, then, and only then will you know what you really want out of life. I call it discovering your authentic self.

Life will give you exactly what you want when you know what you want. You must be perfectly crystal clear about what you want. When you know this, the universe joins in chorus with you to give it to you.

In his classic book, *Think and Grow Rich*, Napoleon Hill wrote about a secret that many successful people have discovered. People attract what they think about. In other words, we are like magnets, constantly attracting opportunities, people, and situations to us. To put it in the terms of an ancient principle: *Like attracts like.*

You attract and become what you hold in your mind both consciously and subconsciously.

As the first of his 17 Principles of Personal Achievement, Napoleon Hill says we have to be clear about what we want. Definiteness of purpose is the starting point of all achievement.

Without a purpose and a plan, people drift aimlessly through life.

Stop focusing on and wasting your energy thinking about what you do not want and start thinking about what you do want! Proverbs 23:7 tells us that as a man thinks in his heart so is he. It also says to guard your heart above all else, for it determines the course of your life (Proverbs 4:23). What do you **really** believe? Look at your life and your beliefs will be staring you in your face.

People often do not have what they want, or do not get what they say with their mouths because they have counter-productive programs running deep within their hearts that broadcast the opposite intentions into the universe. The forces of your past feelings and beliefs put into motion the creative currents that orchestrate the circumstances of your life today. Feelings and thoughts of unworthiness, rejection, and unbelief must not be energized. Whatever has been energized in the past will find ways to manifest in the present and future unless something is done to change what has been energized.

Even though you are speaking truth, truth has not convinced your heart that what you are saying you believe.

Just as we believed in our hearts for salvation, we must have this same belief in our hearts that God has a life of abundance available for us. When I say abundance, I am not necessarily speaking of money or material possessions. We must believe that God has a fulfilling life for us where we serve others, and also enjoy what we do while living in peace and purpose.

Select one of the following exercises which suits you best and begin the process of self-discovery that will drive you forward toward that life you seek.

Exercise 1: Write a letter to your younger self. Choose the age at which you were the most aspiring and had ambitious expectations of life. Explain to that young person how you have gotten to where you are at right now. Describe what has been motivating you and what has been discouraging you. Reveal the details of what you have done with the dreams and desires of that young you. Expound on where you are going now and where you see yourself ending up. How does it feel to that young and inspired you to hear what you are saying on paper now? After this exercise you should be able to say without a doubt what it is that you really want in life.

Tyler Perry, the movie star, film writer, and producer did this exercise and posted it on the internet for all to see. Perry began the letter by acknowledging that his childhood self was going through a tough time in life.

"I know you are having it really hard right now, and you spend a lot of time using your imagination seeing yourself running free in the park and running away from all the pain. In the reflection of your very sad eyes, I see the hurt of watching your mother be belittled and beaten," Perry wrote in the letter. "I see the pain of your own beatings and the insults that you suffer every day. I feel the horror of the hands of the molesters who are trying to rob you of who you are."

Still, Perry let it be known that his faith in God helped give him hope despite the tough times.

"As I search your young face for any sign of myself, believe it or not I'm able to smile. Because just behind all of that darkness I see hope," Perry wrote. "You've got some kind of faith in God little one. I know you don't know this right now but who you've become is being shaped inside of every one of those experiences."

While Perry spoke about the importance of making his mother proud, he also shed light on how God helped him overcome all of the obstacles in his life.

"People are dying all around you, you don't think you'll live to see 30 years old. But there's a still small voice inside of you saying you're going to be okay," Perry wrote. "Looking back on it I know now that that is and was the voice of God. That is the only way to explain how you knew how to navigate your way through turbulent times."

The film mogul ended the letter by revealing that he was proud of himself for all of his success and the ability to beat the odds in his life.

Exercise Two: The Happiest Day in Your Life. The following exercise is designed to activate the mindset of happiness. Get a pen and a piece of paper and describe all the details of what the happiest day in your life would look like. Where would it be? Whom would it be with? What would the circumstances be? What would your health conditions be? What would you be wearing, saying, and doing? Just let your imagination flow freely! Once you are done, you should have some breakthrough ideas about what you really want and what matters most to you in life.

Exercise Three: The Ten Essential Statements that Help You Discover Yourself. It is also highly desirable that you go through the simple questionnaire below and rate each statement on a scale from one to ten.

I am satisfied with myself.

I am happy with the way I look.

I am pleased with my relationships.

I am open to and accept constructive criticism.

I am positive and persistent when times get tough.

I am excited about the successes of other people.

I am fine asking for help or an advice.

I am open-minded and adaptable to change.

I am delighted to meet new people and make connections.

I am aware of myself and guided by my own goals, standards, and values.

How many statements got a ten from you? This exercise should have helped you discover what it is that you really want and need to work toward.

After completing one or more of these exercises you should now have a better understanding of who you are, your authentic self. You should also be better able to clearly identify what you really want out of life.

> **"Our deepest calling is to grow into our own authentic self-hood, whether or not it conforms to some image of who we ought to be. As we do so, we will not only find the joy that every human being seeks--we will also find our path of authentic service in the world." — Parker J. Palmer**

Step Four: Activate Your New Life

Faith is voice activated.

Faith is not a gift like peace, where you simply receive it. Faith takes you actively opening your mouth and speaking what you are expecting to come to pass. Say it until you see it. Speak your new life until you see it. It is not enough to believe it in your heart, you have to say it and then you have to take action and work your plan.

Faith without works is dead. In order to see your life transformed into the life you desire you must activate your faith. You must do things you have never done.

The word, *activate,* means to set in motion; make active or more active. To act is the process of doing or performing something. Whenever you get a new phone or a new debit or credit card you have to activate it. Activating a credit card is fairly easy and you can do so by either going to an ATM machine and swiping your card or by calling the designated telephone number. The point is that you have to do something in order to activate it.

You have to do something in order to get your new life moving forward. Activating your new life is like learning how to ride a bicycle. No matter how beautiful or expensive it is, you have got to get on it, balance yourself, pedal, learn how to use the brakes, and steer all at the same time. It requires specific actions. It is the same with attaining your new life. Believe it, speak it, and then take action to fulfill it.

Step Five: Be Open-Minded

"Change is the law of life. And those who look only to the past or present are certain to miss the fortune." - John F. Kennedy

I must admit that Christians can be some of the most close-minded people on earth. Being open-minded is a necessity to move forward into your new life.

You must be open-minded in order to change how you relate to others, embrace new and innovative ideas and technology, weigh the influence of others, and make mid-course changes or corrections as needed.

A mid-course correction is a navigational correction made in the course of a ship, airplane, rocket, or space vehicle between the beginning and end of the journey. In our lives it could be putting order back in our life again. For those who have experienced defeat and disappointment, it could be coming to grips with the fact that if we do not change it may mean our demise. For those who have been "successful" yet yearn for something more, it means making transformative changes that will catapult you to a new level of success.

In "Mid-Course Correction: Re-Ordering Your Private World for the Second Half of Life," Gordon MacDonald focuses on making choices that lead to personal transformation, significant communal relationships, practical service in the kingdom of God, and a revitalized life of faith and worship. He demonstrates that new significance and meaning are available no matter what your situation has been.

You must always be open to make the necessary changes to advance. No one ever gets to *great* on the first try. It always takes making mid-course corrections.

The 7 Benefits of Being Open-Minded

1. **Letting go of control.** When you open your mind, you free yourself from having to be in complete control of your thoughts. You allow yourself to experience new ideas and thoughts, and you challenge the beliefs you currently have. It can be very liberating to look at the world through an open mind.

2. **Experiencing changes.** Opening up your mind to new ideas allows you the opportunity to change what you think and how you view the world. Now, this does not mean you necessarily *will* change your beliefs, but you have the option to when you think with an open mind.

3. **Making yourself vulnerable.** One of the scariest (and greatest) things about seeing the world through an open mind is making yourself vulnerable. In agreeing to have an open-minded view of the world, you are admitting you do not know everything and that there are possibilities you may not have considered. This vulnerability can be both terrifying and exhilarating.

4. **Making mistakes.** Making mistakes does not seem like it would be much of a benefit, but it truly is. When you open your mind and allow yourself to see things from others' perspectives, you allow yourself not only to recognize potential mistakes you have made, but also to make new mistakes. Does not

sound like much fun, but it is a great thing to fall and get back up again.

5. **Strengthening yourself.** Open-mindedness provides a platform on which you can build, piling one idea on top of another. With an open mind you can learn about new things, and you can use the new ideas to build on the old ideas. Everything you experience can add up, strengthening who you are and what you believe in. It is very hard to build on experiences without an open mind.

6. **Gaining confidence.** When you live with an open mind, you have a strong sense of self. You are not confined by your own beliefs, nor are you confined by the beliefs of others. For that reason, you are able to have and gain confidence as you learn more and more about the world around you. Open-mindedness helps you to learn and grow, strengthening your belief in yourself.

7. **Being honest.** There is an honesty that comes with an open mind because being open-minded means admitting that you are not all-knowing. It means believing that whatever truth you find might always have more to it than you realize. This understanding creates an underlying sense of honesty that permeates the character of anyone who lives with an open mind.

For some, being open-minded is easy; it comes as effortlessly as breathing. For others, having an open mind can be more of a challenge, something that they have to work on and make an effort to attain. You can certainly see from the list above that there are great benefits to viewing life with an open mind. It is not always an easy thing to do, but the effort to think openly and embrace new ideas will be worth it when you are able to take part in the benefits that come from opening your mind.

Step Six: Give

Give and it shall be given to you. What are you willing to give in order to get what you want? There is no getting without first giving. It is the Law of Reciprocity in action. "The Law of Reciprocity is the Universal Law that determines precisely what is received in return, and shows up in physical form as a result of what is broadcast or given out. So the Law of Reciprocity looking at it in this way, requires us to send out or project a vibrational frequency which the Universe, God, Higher Power or whatever you choose to refer to Source as, reciprocates outcomes back to us based on our individual choice as to what we project."[7]

I enjoy peace so I give peace. I enjoy friendship so I am a friend to others. I want love so I give love. There can be no harvest without first planting a seed. This step is crucial. You cannot be stingy with your time, talent or

---

7. http://www.abundance-and-happiness.com/law-of-reciprocity.html

treasure and expect to become abundantly blessed. It does not work that way.

Mother Teresa said, "If you can't feed a hundred people, then just feed one."

Mother Teresa was a Roman Catholic Religious Sister and missionary who founded the Missionaries of Charity, a Roman Catholic religious congregation. In 2012 it consisted of over 4,500 sisters and was active in 133 countries. They run hospices and homes for people with HIV/AIDS, leprosy, and tuberculosis. They host soup kitchens, dispensaries and mobile clinics, children's and family counselling programs, orphanages, and schools. Mother Teresa was the recipient of the 1979 Nobel Peace Prize. She gave unselfishly of herself until the day she died.

"What we have done for ourselves alone dies with us; what we have done for others and the world remains and is immortal," says Albert Pike.

Look at the philanthropic work of some of the wealthiest people in the world. What are you willing to give in return for what you are seeking?

Step Seven: Be All In

Are you willing to do whatever it takes to see your vision come to pass? If you have applied the other six steps in the transformational process, your vision is already in the queue waiting to manifest. This step is designed to keep you on the right path for all of the needed circumstances to fall into place at the right time. It is also designed to make sure that you are willing to do whatever is necessary in order for your life to unfold as you desire. Precision and timing are keys to your success. You must be hungry. You must be able to taste your victory. You must have a desire strong enough to get through any hurdle or obstacle that tries to block you.

I sat spellbound in front of the television as she jumped, leapt, and twirled during her floor rotation. Her unique blend of power, flexibility, body alignment, and form had landed her a spot on the 2012 U.S. Women's Gymnastics team.

Gabrielle Douglas, also fondly known as the Flying Squirrel, is a US Women's Artistic gymnast. At the 2012 London Summer Olympics, she was the first American gymnast to win gold medals in both the team and individual all-around competitions. Gabrielle was the first woman of color of any nationality and the first African-American gymnast in Olympic history to become the Individual All-Around Champion.

We were all intrigued by this young woman who had made sacrifice after sacrifice. Leaving home at age fourteen would be difficult for any child, but this is exactly what Gabby did. When Gabby reached her peak at her local gym, she knew that she needed a new coach who could take her to the Olympic level. She desired to train under elite coach Liang Chow in West Des Moines. After convincing her mother to allow her to move across the country in pursuit of her Olympic dream, and overcoming a number of obstacles placed before her, Gabrielle left Virginia Beach and her family behind to train with Liang Chow.

There is a vetting process that occurs in each of our lives which helps to determine how bad we want something. Whether it is a relationship, a career, or material possessions, our attitude must be such that we will comply with whatever instructions or direction we are receiving as long as it is not illegal, immoral, and hurtful or would compromise our integrity. Listening to and obeying Infinite Intelligence are key in this step.

My husband, Michael, was desperately looking for a job. He had diligently searched the Internet and sent his résumé to company after company. He followed up on every reputable lead that he received only to experience rejection after rejection. He was either overqualified or did not have the required experience. In one experience he had gone through three interviews and was told that he was hired for the job. Days later he was called and told that the company decided that they were going with someone else.

Through a series of events, Michael ended up connecting with a woman who was instrumental in getting him hired for a Fortune 500 company in the food industry, McDonald's. Even though he was hired into the accelerated management program, he still had to work in the restaurant to gain knowledge and information vital to his success in management. He worked hard. He worked every shift and many twelve-to-fourteen-hour days. He knew that he could not advance without following the correct protocol. He knew that he could not sidestep the menial tasks. So he flipped burgers, cooked fries, and took out the trash. He knew, however, that these duties were temporary. He could taste success. He saw himself advancing. He was 100 percent committed to the process. He was all in.

Have you ever heard the phrase, "the fortune is in the follow-up"? It is used regularly in network marketing or sales. I also believe that the fortune is in the follow-through. In this step of the transformation process you must follow through. Making a list of things to do will ensure that you remember everything that you are required to do. Making a list helps you to complete every assignment related to manifesting the life of your dreams. Making a list will also help you ignore the energy-draining distractions that are vying for your attention. It will keep you focused on making the changes necessary to see your life manifest into what you want it to.

"Take up one idea. Make that one idea your life - think of it, dream of it, and live on that idea. Let your brain, muscles, nerves, and every other part of your body be full of that idea, and just leave every other idea alone. This is the way to success, that is way great spiritual giants are produced," says Swami Vivekananda.

Step Eight: Walk in New Beginnings

"Let go of yesterday. Let today be a new beginning and be the best that you can, and you'll get to where God wants you to be." – Joel Osteen

The last step in the Eight-step Transformation Process (8STP) is New Beginnings. It is what I call the come to Jesus moment where you are ready to surrender your life to Infinite Intelligence and you are ready to make the necessary changes to see change

Change is not easy but it is necessary. Making change requires tenacity, focus, and resolve. How long it takes a person to change is totally dependent upon that person. Change can be gradual or instant. Have you ever heard that it takes twenty-one days to make a new habit? I have and thought it was true until I found out that it was a myth. When Dr. Maxwell Maltz wrote his bestselling book, "Psycho Cybernetics," he said that it takes "a minimum of twenty-one days to form a new habit." This phrase was changed and it ended up becoming it takes twenty-one days to form a new habit.

On average, it takes more than two months before a new behavior becomes automatic—sixty-six days to be exact. How long it takes a new habit to form can vary widely depending on the behavior, the person, and the circumstances. In Phillippa Lally's study, it took anywhere from eighteen to 254 days for people to form a new habit. In other words, if you want to set your expectations appropriately, the truth is that it will probably take you anywhere from two months to eight months to build a new behavior into your life—not twenty-one days.

Do not become discouraged if you do not see immediate change. Keep working at it and remember Rome was not built in a day.

Retraining Your Brain

Dr. Caroline Leaf is a cognitive neuroscientist specializing in Neuropsychology which is a branch of psychology that is concerned with how the brain and the rest of the nervous system influence a person's cognition and behaviors. I became acquainted with Dr. Leaf when I heard her teaching on the subject of Neuroplasticity which **refers to the lifelong capacity of the brain to change and rewire itself in response to the stimulation of learning and experience.**

Years ago scientists thought that our brains were hardwired from birth and that because of genetics our destiny was set. Today research has shown us differently. You can break toxic thinking and reverse its affects. This process is called neuroplasticity. This is incredible news. No matter how toxic a person's thinking is, when they commit to making positive changes in their lives, it is possible. When toxic thinking is broken you can expect to change every area of your life.

For some walking in new beginnings is a matter of life and death, literally. If your patterns of thinking are worrying, fear, doubt, and anger changing to a more positive mindset is essential for living a healthier and happier life.

Toxic thoughts are like poison. They put extreme strain on your body's systems that can result in everything from patchy memory to severe mental health issues, immune system problems, heart problems, and digestive problems. Research has determined that 80 percent of physical, emotional, and mental health issues could be the direct result of your thought lives.

Walk in new beginnings. Choose life and live. Start living your new life today.

"Change is hard because people overestimate the value of what they have—and underestimate the value of what they may gain by giving that up." — James Belasco and Ralph Stayer, *Flight of the Buffalo* (1994)

Key Points

You attract and become what you hold in your mind both consciously and subconsciously.

Without a purpose and a plan, people drift aimlessly through life.

Even though you are speaking truth, truth has not convinced your heart that what you are saying you believe.

"Our deepest calling is to grow into our own authentic self-hood, whether or not it conforms to some image of who we ought to be. As we do so, we will not only find the joy that every human being seeks--we will also find our path of authentic service in the world." — Parker J. Palmer

Faith is voice activated.

You must always be open to make the necessary changes to advance. No one ever gets to great on the first try. It always takes making mid-course corrections.

"What we have done for ourselves alone dies with us; what we have done for others and the world remains and is immortal," says Albert Pike.

Discovery Action Steps

You must be hungry.

You must be able to taste your victory.

You must have a desire strong enough to get through any hurdle or obstacle that tries to block you.

Which of these characteristics describe you?

Which ones do you need to work on?

"Take up one idea. Make that one idea your life - think of it, dream of it, and live on that idea. Let your brain, muscles, nerves, and every other part of your body be full of that idea, and just leave every other idea alone. This is the way to success, that is way great spiritual giants are produced," says Swami Vivekananda.

Are you ready to commit to following **The Eight-step Transformation Process?**

Check them off as you complete each step.

- Step One: Know The Truth
- Step Two: Transform Your Mind
- Step Three: Determine What You Really Want
- Step Four: Activate Your New
- Step Five: Be Open-Minded
- Step Six: Give
- Step Seven: Be All In
- Step Eight: Walk in New Beginnings

CHAPTER 13
Regaining My Confidence after a Setback

"There is no easy walk to freedom anywhere, and many of us will have to pass through the valley of the shadow of death again and again before we reach the mountaintop of our desires." - Nelson Mandela

Valley Lessons

> *"Listen carefully: Unless a grain of wheat is buried in the ground, dead to the world, it is never any more than a grain of wheat. But if it is buried, it sprouts and reproduces itself many times over. In the same way, anyone who holds on to life just as it is destroys that life. But if you let it go, reckless in your love, you'll have it forever, real and eternal." (John 12:24-25)*

Chippie the parakeet never saw it coming. One second he was peacefully perched in his cage. The next he was sucked in, washed up, and blown over. The problems began when Chippie's owner decided to clean Chippie's cage with a vacuum cleaner. She removed the attachment from the end of the hose and stuck it in the cage. The phone rang, and she turned to pick it up. She had barely said "hello" when Chippie got sucked in. The bird owner gasped, put down the phone, turned off the vacuum, and opened the bag. There was Chippie—still alive, but stunned.

Since the bird was covered with dust and soot, she grabbed him and raced to the bathroom, turned on the faucet, and held Chippie under the running water. Then, realizing that Chippie was soaked and shivering, she did what any compassionate bird owner would do, she reached for the hair dryer and blasted the pet with hot air.

Poor Chippie never knew what hit him. A few days after the trauma, the reporter who had initially written about the event contacted Chippie's owner to see how the bird was recovering.

"Well," she replied, "Chippie does not sing much anymore—he just sits and stares."

It is not hard to see why. Sucked in, washed up, and blown over. That is enough to steal the song from the stoutest heart.

Chippies story is my story and yours. Battered, scarred, and left for dead from divorce to sickness, job loss to the death of a loved one. Each one of us has a story. It is one thing when you do not have control over things that happen to you as a child or an elderly person or someone incapable of fending for themselves. It is another thing when we allow life to happen to us, and when we do not take responsibility for our actions. Do not be like Chippie. Rise again and start singing.

The truth is everyone will have challenges and setbacks, and we are exactly where we are supposed to be based on the decisions that we have made.

"Into each life some rain must fall but too much is fallin' in mine," are the lyrics to a song. Have you ever wondered why bad things happen to good people? Why do the good ones seem to endure such tremendous hardships? The truth of the matter is that no one is exempt from experiencing challenging seasons in their lives. No one will go through their life with everything coming up roses. There are times in life where everything *is* really just excellent, life is prosperous, and everything you touch turns to gold! The premise of this book is that you can create the life of your dreams by managing your thoughts, actions, and deeds, and that you can live the good life if you are willing to put in the time and discipline needed.

However, no one is exempt from challenges and setbacks.

The greatest achievers say that in a lifetime of setbacks and comebacks, the truest sense of accomplishment is not found in the realization of the goal, but rather in the will to continue when failure breeds doubt.[8] Here are ten people who bounced back after a setback in their lives. One thing they all had in common was they never gave up.

Napoleon Hill was an American author in the area of the new thought movement who was one of the earliest producers of the modern genre of personal-success literature. He is widely considered to be one of the great writers on success. His most famous work, *Think and Grow Rich* (1937), is one of the best-selling books of all time.

Napoleon endured setback after setback. He overcame being broke, destitute, fleeing for his life, divorced, and met disappointment and failure before attaining success.

George Washington Carver was an American scientist, botanist, educator, and inventor. Carver's reputation is based on his research into and promotion of alternative crops to cotton, such as peanuts, soybeans, and sweet potatoes which also aided nutrition for farm families. Carver was born into slavery in Diamond Grove, Missouri and was kidnapped immediately after birth. However, he had an insatiable desire to learn and attended a school ten miles from home. He relocated many times during his youth. Carver applied to several colleges before being accepted at Highland College in Highland, Kansas.

---

8. See more at: http://www.success.com/article/rich-man-poor-man#sthash.Z1YTYd6I.dpuf

When he arrived, however, they rejected him because of his race.

Esther, a Jewish orphan girl, was raised by her cousin, Mordecai. Esther became queen of Persia and thwarted a plan to commit genocide against her people.

Bill Gates' first business failed. Yes, the richest person in the whole world could not make any money at first. Traf-O-Data (a device which could read traffic tapes and process the data), failed miserably. When Gates and his partner, Paul Allen, tried to sell it, the product would not even work.

Albert Einstein did not speak until he was four years old and did not have the best childhood. In fact, many people thought he was just a dud. Throughout elementary school many of his teachers thought he was lazy and would not make anything of himself. He always received good marks, but his head was in the clouds, conjuring up abstract questions people could not understand. He kept thinking and eventually developed the theory of relativity, which many of us still cannot wrap our heads around.

Oprah Winfrey is one of the most successful and richest people in the world today, but Winfrey did not always have it so easy. She grew up in Milwaukee, Wisconsin and was repeatedly molested by her cousin, uncle, and a family friend. She eventually ran away from home, and at the age of fourteen gave birth to a baby boy who died shortly after his birth. Winfrey's tragic past did not stop her from becoming the force she is today. She excelled as an honor's student in high school, and won an oratory contest which secured her a full scholarship to college. Now the entrepreneur and personality has the admiration of millions and a net worth of $2.9 billion.

Vincent Van Gogh is considered one of the greatest artists of all time, yet the poor guy only sold one painting the entire time he was alive: "The Red Vineyard at Arles (The Vigne Rouge)," which is now in the Pushkin Museum of Fine Arts in Moscow. Even though he made no money, he still painted over 900 works of art. Though his persistence went unnoticed when he was alive, Van Gogh proves you do not need external validation to be proud of the work you create.

Bethany Hamilton started surfing when she was just a child. At age thirteen, an almost deadly shark attack resulted in her losing her left arm. She was back on her surfboard one month later, and two years after that, she won first place in the Explorer Women's Division of the NSSA National Championships. Talk about determination.

Why Setbacks?

The *Urban Dictionary* online defines setback as something that keeps you from doing something and can cause great inconvenience to someone's life. A setback may just knock you off your time schedule or it could be stopping you from doing something you drastically need to do. Setbacks are not good, most of the time.

The *Free Dictionary* defines setback as an unanticipated or sudden check in progress; a change from better to worse; an unfortunate happening that hinders or impedes; something that is thwarting or frustrating.

Anything that takes you off of your course and purpose is a setback. A setback is a hindrance or problem that interrupts your progress. It is usually temporary, an unanticipated or sudden check in progress, or a change from better to worse.

The loss of a loved one, a divorce, sickness, cancer, moving, a job change, bankruptcy, foreclosure, and becoming a caregiver are events that have the potential to cause a setback or are setbacks themselves. There has never been one person who has walked the earth who has not encountered at least one setback in their lifetime. We live in the "real" world and are not a part of the Truman show living in the cheerful community of Seahaven, an island "paradise" where the weather is always mild and no unpleasantness intrudes. We are constantly bombarded with news and situations which could keep us in the mode of a setback.

There are different reasons that we go through heartache, hardship, setbacks, and challenges with the most obvious being they are all a part of life. One of the most obvious reasons in that life is comprised of experiences—some good and some bad, some happy and some sad. We lose loved ones, we get divorced, we get sick, we get fired, and we lose possessions.

Pruning is a horticultural process involving the selective removal of parts of a plant such as branches, buds, or roots. Reasons to prune plants include deadwood removal, shaping (by controlling or directing growth), improving or maintaining health, reducing risk from falling branches, preparing nursery specimens for transplanting, and both harvesting and increasing the yield or quality of flowers and fruits. The practice entails *targeted* removal of diseased, damaged, dead, non-productive, structurally unsound, or otherwise unwanted tissue from crop and landscape plants.

At first glance, pruning may seem to be a counter-intuitive activity because what you are pruning would seem to most as a very healthy vine. However, it is not just the removal of what is dead.

Pruning can also mean cutting away the good and the better so that we might enjoy the best.

The television show "Hoarders Alive" is a documentary about the real life struggles and treatment of people who suffer from compulsive hoarding. Compulsive hoarding (more accurately described as "hoarding disorder") is a pattern of behavior that is characterized by the excessive acquisition of and inability or unwillingness to discard large quantities of objects that cover the living areas of the home and cause significant distress or impairment. The reason I bring up hoarding is that we can be hoarders of physical things that overrun our homes and prevent us from moving around, but we can be just as guilty of brain hoarding—holding on to destructive, toxic thought and imaginations.

We can be guilty of hoarding negative thoughts that make it very hard to get anything positive into our brains.

"Digged and Dunged" is an interesting sermon I heard taught by W. Max Alderman concerning the parable of the fig tree in Luke 13: 6-9.[9]

He spake also this parable; A certain man had a fig tree planted in his vineyard; and he came and sought fruit thereon, and found none. Then said he unto the dresser of his vineyard, Behold, these three years I come seeking fruit on this fig tree, and find none: cut it down; why cumbereth it the ground? And he answering said unto him, Lord, let it alone this year also, till I shall dig about it, and dung it: And if it bear fruit, well: and if not, then after that thou shalt cut it down. (KJV)

Do you need a good "digging and dunging"? Sometimes, as a result of dealing with the cares of life we become bitter, resentful, and unfruitful. Our hearts become hard, fallow, and we become barren. The vine dresser suggests that we are salvageable and offers to turn over the hard places in

---

9. http://www.sermoncentral.com/sermons/wll-god-have-to-dig-and-dung-you-w-alderman-sermon-on-christian-witness-130678.asp?Page=1

our lives and nourish us by a process called "digging and dunging." If you have been planted in the vineyard of God, know that it is a very special place and that you have been given special treatment. You are favored. Allow the Holy Spirit to work on you. Give up the malice! Forgive those who hurt you. Stop being angry. Stop speaking negatively. Get over "it" and move on. Read the Word of God, pray, and get that much needed nourishment today.

Overcoming a Major Setback

Breakdowns can create breakthroughs. Things fall apart so things can fall together.

One thing I have learned, having come through many setbacks myself, is if you do not move forward after a setback you will always be "set back." You will **never** be who God intended you to be. Another thing that I have learned is you must accept it. Whether it is a relationship that has failed or a financial setback or a health challenge, acceptance is necessary in order to properly deal with it.

Living in denial will only intensify your pain and cause your healing to de delayed. You can come back after a setback if you confront it, thereby bringing resolution and resolve.

There are five "A-s" that can keep you moving ahead and help you overcome a major setback in your life.

Acknowledge: Acknowledging that something has gone terribly wrong and realizing that you need to make some mid-course correction is one of the hardest things to do especially after a major setback. However, if not done it could cause what is bad to become even worse or irreparable.

Align: When we go through tough times it is imperative that we have the right people in our circles of influence. Align yourself with people who will encourage and inspire you out of your dark place.

Accentuate: Accentuate the positives and minimize the negatives.

Articulate: Articulate your vision. Say it out loud. Speak positive and good things about yourself. Open your mouth and proclaim your vision.

Accelerate: Get out of the setback as soon as you can. Do not stay there and wallow in it. Shake the dust off of your feet and keep it moving. Be they ever so small, even baby steps are important. Just keep moving ahead.

Getting Back on Track

Once you are ready to make your comeback just do it! There are many things in life that you cannot change! Accept them and move on. Change what you can! Be your authentic self! Love God and people and enjoy life! Do not let life pass you by trying to fix things that you cannot fix and change people that you cannot change. Find your Happy Place and run to it!

Do not spin your wheels trying to fix things that you cannot fix.

The Serenity Prayer says, "God grant me the serenity to accept the things I cannot change; courage to change the things I can; and wisdom to know the difference."

So you have recovered from a setback and are now ready to get back in the game. You have heard everyone's opinions and now you must decide what is best for you. Now how do you get back in the game? This process can be tricky and requires that you move very strategically. It must be well thought out and you must count the cost of every decision that you make. I had a major setback which turned out to be a tremendous set up.

I experienced a major setback while on vacation in Nashville, Tennessee. My husband, Michael and our youngest son, Solomon drove to Nashville to spend the 4th of July. We were very excited and were anticipating a fun, stress free, and uneventful time. Needless to say, this vacation was far from that.

After researching the website of Diners, Drive-Ins, and Dives looking for a nice place to eat, we discovered that one of the restaurants was about fifteen miles away. Michael, Solomon, and I set out to visit it. It was a rainy but pleasant day. Upon arrival we were invited to sit on the porch of the restaurant to wait until there was a table available for us. I was feeling great and enjoyed the conversation of the ladies who we sat near while waiting for our names to be called.

After about thirty minutes our name was called and we were escorted to our table. We were so excited about being at a restaurant featured on Diners, Drive-Ins, and Dives. The restaurant was quaint and every inch of the homelike environment was filled. We placed our order and were given biscuits to enjoy while we waited. When our food arrived it looked delicious, we could hardly wait to dig in.

After several bites I began to experience heart palpitations. I just knew that everyone was looking at me. My heart was beating so hard and rapidly it felt as though it was going to jump right out of my chest. I had never had this feeling before. I excused myself and went to the restroom. As I walked into the restroom I thought I was going to pass out. The feeling of anxiety that I was experiencing grew worse. Upon returning to our table I announced to my husband that we needed to leave immediately. I tried to remain calm so as not to upset our son or my husband, but by this time I was feeling really bad and hiding the truth of how I felt was hard.

We proceeded to pay our bill and to make our way to the car. I did not want to go to the hospital so I tried to refocus my attention on the scenery along the route back to the hotel. It did not work. My husband knew that I was not doing well. We went back to our hotel and decided that if I was not better within thirty minutes that we would find and visit the nearest Emergency Room. After about twenty minutes in the room, I told Michael that I needed to go to the hospital. He had already selected a hospital and was trying to figure out how to get there. I was thinking to myself, what a way to spend our vacation.

When we arrived at hospital, we were seen right away. Anytime anyone shares with the intake worker that they are having heart palpitations they are seen right away. I guess that they did not know if it was a heart attack or what. I knew that it was not. I was not experiencing any shortness of breath or chest pains, but there was definitely something wrong.

I was seen by a doctor immediately and my heart rate was taken. It was almost twice the normal rate that it should have been. I was thinking, as soon as my heart goes back into normal range I am out of here. Wrong!

After seeing the cardiologist and the endocrinologist and having test after test, my diagnosis was in. It was surmised that I had gone from hypothyroidism to hyperthyroidism, and that my blood pressure was out of whack. It was further diagnosed that I had hypertrophic cardiomyopathy or in layman's terms a "thick" heart.

Hypertrophic cardiomyopathy (HCM) is a condition in which the heart muscle becomes thick. Often only one part of the heart is thicker than the other parts. The thickening can make it harder for blood to leave the heart, forcing the heart to work harder to pump blood. It also can make it harder for the heart to relax and fill with blood.

Hypertrophic cardiomyopathy is a condition that is usually passed down through families or inherited. It is believed to be a result of several problems or defects with the genes that control heart muscle growth.

Younger people are likely to have a more severe form of hypertrophic cardiomyopathy. However, the condition is seen in people of all ages. Some patients have no symptoms. They may not even realize they have the condition until it is found during a routine medical exam. The first symptom of hypertrophic cardiomyopathy among many young patients is sudden collapse and possible death. This can be caused by very abnormal heart rhythms called arrhythmias, or from the blockage of blood from the heart to the rest of the body.[10]

Upon hearing this diagnosis I was thinking, *What is going on? Do I have a heart condition where I can drop dead at any moment?* I could not believe my ears. I was hooked up to a heart monitor, I had an IV, and I could not even go the restroom alone. As I lay there I kept wondering what I had gotten myself into. I sincerely wished I had never agreed to come to the emergency room. They admitted me. I was finally discharged after two days with three medicines in hand I was instructed to take.

Though I knew I had to take it easy for a while, I also knew that I could not just allow my diagnosis to debilitate me. It took a while, but I finally got my strength back and began going to the gym two or three times a week.

---

10. http://www.nlm.nih.gov/medlineplus/ency/article/000192.htm

I also started speaking life to my body. I meditated on what I could do and I did not dwell on negativity. I did not allow myself to reiterate or keep rehearsing the doctor's diagnosis.

My experience could have been a major setback in my life had I allowed it to cripple me. It could have made me fearful and steal my dreams. Instead I have used it to motivate me to stay on my quest to feeling better and losing weight. To date I have lost forty pound and lots of inches. I am a happy girl. To see how I did it and got myself back in shape you can go to my website at www.totallifechanges.com/adudley.

Use what was meant for evil to thrust you forward in your destiny. Make a decision to move past every setback.

Key Points

The truth is everyone will have challenges and setbacks, and we are exactly where we are supposed to be based on the decisions that we have made.

No one is exempt from challenges and setbacks.

Pruning can also mean cutting away the good and the better so that we might enjoy the best.

We can be guilty of hoarding negative thoughts that make it very hard to get anything positive into our brains.

Breakdowns can create breakthroughs. Things fall apart so things can fall together.

Do not spin your wheels trying to fix things that you cannot fix.

Discovery Action Steps

Check off these steps as you move yourself forward after a major setback.

- **Acknowledge** that you need to make some mid-course change.
- **Align** yourself with people who will encourage and inspire you out of your dark place.
- **Accentuate** the positives and minimize the negatives.
- **Articulate** your vision. Say it out loud. Speak positive and good things about yourself. Open your mouth and proclaim your vision.
- **Accelerate** and get out of the setback as soon as you can.

CHAPTER 14
Maintaining Your Authenticity

Earlier in the book we talked about the need to discover your authentic self. Once you have found the authentic you, you do not want to lose you again. However, maintaining your authenticity may be a bit more challenging than you think. The pressures of life weigh us down and try to make us "fit in" with the status quo. Being authentic takes work, determination, and a defined purpose or a true understanding of who you are in the universe. It is easy to morph into something or someone you were not created to be.

Maintaining your authenticity is of absolute necessity if you are going to rule your world.

Nine Steps to Live True to Yourself

Step #1: Do You. *I encourage you to j*ourney to the center of you. Stop making apologies for who God created you to be. There is a phrase that says, "Get in Where You Fit in." I would like to coin another phrase and say, "Get in If You

Fit in." There are certain situations that will compromise your authenticity if you make yourself "fit" in. Finding where you fit in allows you to be you. If you do not fit in, do not beat yourself up about it. Keep looking. Your "tribe" is looking for you. They are seeking you just as much as you are seeking them.

I attended a seminar in Detroit hosted by Bishop Corletta Vaughn. The special guest was First Lady Myesha Chaney, wife of one of the preachers from LA. She was on the "Hiding Behind the Lipstick" book tour where she was also the guest speaker. At the end of the presentation she offered each woman an opportunity to write the things that have held her back or hindered her. It was called their "lipstick" confession. She then invited those women who were brave to share their lipstick confessions with the group. Several women shared and vowed to stop hiding behind their lipstick and live in their authenticity and purpose.

Be brave and true to who you are. Stop wearing unnecessary masks just to fit in or avoid facing the reality of who you are. Those masks can make life feel hopeless and imprisoning! Even in a crowd of faces, it is easy to feel lonely if we are not being ourselves, and if the people around us do not appreciate who we really are.

Refuse to give up your seat of authenticity.

Come to the front of the bus. When you are yourself, you not only invite others to do the same, you become a bright watch tower for the people you wish would find you.

Step #2: Step into the Wilderness. Michael and I lived in Adrian, Michigan for several years. I call those my wilderness years, my Egypt experience. During wilderness experiences you find out who you really, what you are made of, and your destiny is often revealed and magnified. You become vulnerable, naked, humble, and you are forced to face your fears. The enemy of your destiny lives in the wilderness waiting to pounce on you. He offers you a life of grandeur if you will just comprise who you are. He wants you to bow down, serve, and follow him. Mediocrity lives in the wilderness as do lack, drought, and fear. You are encouraged to deny your destiny in your wilderness. The wilderness is dry and hot, and dehydration is imminent if you do not find water. The tempter lives in the wilderness and says he will give you anything that you want if you will forget this nonsense of doing what you were created to do. In the midst of temptation you can find peace if you will stay within your authenticity. Remember, the tempter is a fraud.

A fraud cannot offer you authenticity.

"The clearest way into the Universe is through a forest wilderness." — John Muir

Step #3 – Infinite Intelligence Is Speaking. *Are you listening?* Your life's purpose has already been discovered. Listen closely to the conversation that is going on inside of you. The more you pay attention to this conversation the more you will want to listen. It takes practice to hear this guidance just as it takes practice to hear your heart's desire, to trust your gut, and to listen to your intuition. Infinite Intelligence leaves clues. These clues are what will lead you along destiny's path. You have the ability to live a life that is true to who you are and a life that you really want. Listen like your life depends on it.

"Creativity comes from trust. Trust your instincts."
— *Rita Mae Brown*

Step #4: Count the Cost and Do it. Make choices that put you above everything and everyone else, even those you love and cherish the most. If you do not take care of yourself, if you do not do what is best for you, your relationships will eventually suffer. Trust in the fact that doing what is best for you *is* best for everyone even if it does not feel like it at first. Sometimes sacrifices have to made. People will get hurt and there will be losses, but the rewards gained from following your heart are absolutely everything in comparison. Do something difficult for no other reason than that you like to do it.

"Every day we have plenty of opportunities to get angry, stressed or offended. But what you're doing when you indulge these negative emotions is giving something outside yourself power over your happiness. You can choose to not let little things upset you." - **Joel Osteen**

Step #5: Believe. Whatever you think is your truth. Let me paraphrase what Henry Ford said. If you think you can, you are probably right. If you think you cannot, you are probably right. Belief in yourself is essential to living authentically. Many people fail because they give up before they even try. Do not stop believing in yourself even for one second. You have to push beyond unbelief, doubt, and fear. Unbelief cannot hide. It is out in full view. When you believe in yourself you exude a certain aura. You attract success. Even if your towel is sweaty or filled with tears, do not throw it away. Persevere! Keep believing no matter what.

"Some people say I have attitude—maybe I do, but I think you have to. You have to believe in yourself when no one else does—that makes you a winner right there." - Venus Williams

Step #6: *I am Not My Hair.* In America a great deal of value is placed on our outer appearance, especially if you are an African-American woman. It is very important to get clear on the fact that you are more, so much more than how you look. India Arie penned a song titled, "I am not my hair." Here are some of the lyrics of the song:

"Does the way I wear my hair make me a better person? Does the way I wear my hair make me a better friend?

Does the way I wear my hair determine my integrity? I am expressing my creativity...

Breast Cancer and Chemotherapy Took away her crown and glory She promised God if she was to survive She would enjoy every day of her life On national television Her diamond eyes are sparkling Bald headed like a full moon shining Singing out to the whole wide world like, HEY."

You see it is never been about how you look—your shape, your color, your race or even your hair. You are not your hair. It is about the light that illuminates from within. Let your light shine so that others will be drawn to that light and worship the giver of that light.

Michael and I traveled the United States on a bus in a singing group called, Festival of Praise. Every Sunday we performed two concerts in two different churches in two cities in close proximity to each other. After the evening performance we would all wait excitedly to see who we would be paired with hoping to be selected to go to some luxurious home for the night with an aristocratic looking family with two children, an able bodied mom and dad with a dog and a cat. Well, let's leave the dog and cat out since I am allergic to both.

One particular Sunday evening they said, "Michael and Andrea, you are going home with the assistant pastor and his wife. To our dismay in our small mindedness, he was about four foot nine and a paraplegic. He could not even help us with our luggage. He and his wife lived on the campus of the church so we did not have very far to go. We were glad for that.

That night staying in their modest abode was a life changing experience for us, so much so that the residue of his impact lingers on even today. That man ministered to us so very profoundly that we vowed to never, ever judge a person by how they looked ever again. We were ashamed and convicted of how we pre-judged this giant of a man. He was living his truth in his authenticity, and it changed our lives. Monday morning we awakened, received our bag lunch, began our travels all over again, and were grateful for the opportunity to have met this precious soul. The light that illuminated from him burned so brightly that his being a paraplegic was a non-factor.

"Beauty is not in the face; beauty is a light in the heart."
— Khalil Gibran

Do not allow how you look to limit what you do. Allow your light to shine brightly and live out your truth.

Step #7: **You Are the Master of Your Own Fate.** Everyone is born into a family. Sometimes the environment from which we are raised places limits and boundaries upon us which must be broken. Break free. Do not allow the limitations of your parents to hold you back. You have the power within to do whatever you set your mind to do. Use your foundation as a spring board to thrust you forward.

You **are the architect of your existence.**

"Every great dream begins with a dreamer. Always remember, you have within you the strength, the patience, and the passion to reach for the stars to change the world."
— Harriet Tubman

Step #8: Become Whole—Nothing Broken, Nothing Missing. Love you flaws and all. The healing salve of love will heal your soul, your body, and your spirit. Every experience, good and bad creates, the fabric of your life. Your experiences shape you. When you accept that you are where you are in life because of the decisions that you have made, you give yourself permission to change. Hurts, disappointments, and pain no longer paint the canvas of your life when you live in your authenticity. The Creator of the universe loves you with an everlasting love. When you accept this love, you open yourself up to live and to love.

Wholeness awaits you. Open and receive.

"A man cannot be comfortable without his own approval." **– Mark Twain**

Step #9: Enter into His Rest. I have trouble resting. Sometimes my mind is racing with thoughts and ideas which are filled with emotions. I have to purposefully and intentionally bring my thoughts to quietness.

A rested mind can tap into your authenticity.

Living authentically means living in the purpose for which you were created. It means trusting that your Creator has your back. One of the definitions of relax is to become less firm. So then relaxing your grip on your own life, career, family, etc., and giving them over to God in faith is the best way to relax. Your mind may be shouting a list of all of things that you need to do, but simply ignore it and rest. Erase your agenda. Clear your mind. Rest.

So God blessed the seventh day and made it holy, because on it God rested from all his work that he had done in creation. (Genesis 2:3)

Key Points

Maintaining your authenticity is of absolute necessity if you are going to rule your world.

Refuse to give up your seat of authenticity.

A fraud cannot offer you authenticity.

Do not allow how you look to limit what you do. Allow your light to shine brightly and live out your truth.

You are the architect of your existence.

Wholeness awaits you. Open and receive.

A rested mind can tap into your authenticity.

Discovery Action Steps

Step #1: Do You. Journey to the center of you. Stop making apologies for who God created you to be. Be brave and true to who you are. Stop wearing unnecessary masks just to fit in or avoid facing the reality of who you are.

Step #2: Step into the Wilderness. During wilderness experiences you find out who you really, what you are made of, and your destiny is often revealed and magnified.

You become vulnerable, naked, humble, and you face your fears.

Step #3: Infinite Intelligence Is Speaking. It takes practice to hear this guidance as it takes practice to hear your heart's desire, to trust your gut, and to listen to your intuition. Listen like your life depends on it.

Step #4: Count the Cost and Do it. Make choices that put you above everything and everyone else.

Step #5: Believe. If you think you can, you are probably right. If you think you cannot, you are probably right. Belief in yourself is essential to living authentically.

Step #6 – I am Not My Hair. It is very important to get clear on the fact that you are more, so much more than how you look. Do not allow how you look to limit what you do. Allow your light to shine brightly and live out your truth.

Step #7: You Are the Master of Your Own Fate. Sometimes the environment from which we are raised places limits and boundaries upon us which must be broken. You have the power within to do whatever you set your mind to do. *You* are the architect of your existence.

Step #8: Become Whole—Nothing Broken, Nothing Missing. Love you flaws and all. When you accept that you are where you are in life because of the decisions that you have made, you give yourself permission to change.

Step #9: Enter into His Rest. A rested mind can tap into your authenticity. Living authentically means living in the purpose for which you were created. It means trusting that your Creator has your back. Erase your agenda. Clear your mind. Rest.

Conclusion

What Is Next? Write Your Own Obituary

"The value of life is not in its duration, but in its donation. You are not important because of how long you live, you are important because of how effective you live. And most people are concerned about growing old rather than being effective." — Dr. Myles Munroe

You will have to be very brave and courageous in order to complete this last assignment. I had never thought about writing my own obituary until I heard Dr. Munroe, in a television interview prior to his death, talk about writing his own obituary. I thought, how morbid until I did the research, then I understood the concept.

Writing your own obituary is a common exercise assigned by life coaches. It is to be written how you would like it to be one day. This allows you to really look at what you would like your life to include, where you would like to be, and what achievements are really important for you to pursue for your own peace of mind.

Most Wanted Outcome

When writing a book there is a formula used to determine what the author wants the outcome of the book to be. It is called the "Most Wanted Outcome." The author is asked to think about what are the ingredients that they need to include in order to create the kind of book they want. They are to list what needs to be included in the book in order for their readers to get the desired outcome. In other words, they need to define what the most wanted outcome for them as the writer and the most wanted outcome for their readers as well.

You have an authentic gift or calling that you were born to fulfill. It takes living with intention to live the life you were born to live.

What is your most wanted outcome for you? What do you want others to say about how you lived and about the legacy you have left in the earth?

In my research of writing your own obituary, I found this article. After reading it, I trust that you will have a better understanding of it.

Wake-Up Call: Write Your Obituary

(Lifestyle by Marelisa Fabrega)

"Alfred Nobel, the inventor of dynamite, was reading the newspaper one morning when, to his shock, he turned the page and discovered his obituary inside. It turns out that his brother had died, and the newspaper had published

Alfred's obituary by mistake. The obituary read, "The merchant of death is dead. Dr. Alfred Nobel, who became rich by finding ways to kill more people faster than ever before, died yesterday."

Needless to say, Nobel was taken aback by the way in which the world was going to remember him after his death. It's believed that it was due to this shock that Nobel decided to set aside the bulk of his estate in order to establish the Nobel Foundation, which annually bestows international awards in recognition of cultural and scientific advances. Today, Nobel is not remembered as the merchant of death, but as the creator of the Nobel Prizes, and, consequently, as a great humanitarian. Having read his obituary while he was still alive gave him the opportunity to change his legacy.

Although it sounds a bit macabre, writing your own obituary—or asking a friend or a family member to do it for you—can be an excellent wake-up call that can help you make important changes in your life."

Let's Do It

Write an obituary as a true account of your life to date. As an alternative, you can ask a friend or family member who knows you well to do it for you. When it is ready, look over your obituary and ask yourself the following questions.

- *If I died today, would I die happy?*
- *Am I satisfied with the direction in which my life is headed?*

- *Am I happy with the legacy that I am creating?*
- *What is missing from my life?*
- *What do I need to do in order for my obituary to be "complete"?*

Then write a fictional obituary in which you write down all of the things you wish you had done with your life.

What did you discover from this exercise? You have not kicked the bucket yet, so get out there and start ruling your world. Start making any changes that you need to so that you can "live up" to your fictional obituary.

Power to Change

You are where you are today based on past decisions. You have the power to rule your world. Choose wisely today because tomorrow you will reap the harvest of the seeds that you sow today. Decide the kind of life that you want to live, and start making choices that will produce the abundant, peaceful, and secure life that you want.

If you do not like your life, make a mid-course correction and change the direction you are going. It is as simple as that. A chain of positive, good choices will give you a positive, good life.

Remember, Infinite Intelligence wants to help you. Ask Infinite Intelligence to lead, guide, and direct you. You will find that no matter what you encounter you will always come out stronger and wiser.

Acknowledgements

Life is all about movement, change and transition. When things would happen in my life, my dad, Lessley, used to always say, "That's Life". In other words life is filled with moving parts and the sooner that you understand this lesson, the better you'll do in life. I owe my parents monumental thanks for providing me with the solid foundation on which I was raised. Their love and support taught me to deal with change. I also learned from them that I must always be true to who God created me to be.

No matter what I do, I always have his support. He is always there to encourage me to go after my dreams. He is always there to ignite my fire. He is my best friend and husband, Michael Thomas Dudley. Thank you for your ever-increasing patience, your love, and your commitment. I love you.

I asked the Holy Spirit for a writing and publishing coach and he gave me Dr. Larry Keefauver. When I released this request, I did not have a clue how it would manifest.

Briefly, here is how it happened.

I sat next to a man on a flight to Dallas, Texas to attend a funeral. Upon arriving to my seat I attempted to put my super heavy carry-on luggage in the overhead bin. This gentleman asked if I needed help.

Upon lifting the bag he said, "Boy this bag is heavy, what do you have in it?"

"Books," I said. "I am a speaker and I will make them available to anyone who wants to purchase them after I minister on Sunday."

Little did I know that God had answered my prayer! I had no idea that I was sitting next to "the" one and only Dr. Larry Keefauver. For the next three hours he poured into me, inspired me, and encouraged me. I was in awe at how the Holy Spirit had so graciously answered my prayer. I was grateful.

Please allow me to share with you some of his credentials and you will see how majorly God blessed me when he brought Dr. Keefauver into my life.

Dr. Larry Keefauver, with degrees from the University of Pennsylvania and Texas Christian University, is professionally and educationally trained in pastoral counseling. His wife Judi is a registered nurse. He and his wife have written best-selling family books which include: *Lord I Wish My Family Would Get Saved*, *The 77 Irrefutable Truths of Parenting* (with Judi), *Proactive Parenting—The Early Years*, *The 77 Irrefutable Truths of Marriage* (with Judi), *Lord I Wish My Teenage Would Talk With Me*, and *Lord I Wish My*

Husband Would Pray with Me. Judi's devotional book for women is *Be*.

With over 2.5 million books worldwide in over 11 languages, Dr. Keefauver is the noted author of *Inviting God's Presence, When God Doesn't Heal Now, Experiencing the Holy Spirit, The 77 Irrefutable Truths of Ministry, Hugs for Grandparents, Hugs for Heroes, Commanding Angels—Invoking the Standing Orders, From the Oval Office: Prayers of the Presidents, The 77 Irrefutable Truths of Prayer,* and *Friend to Friend*.

Dr. Keefauver, words cannot express my heartfelt appreciation to you for helping me to complete my first solo project. I am forever and eternally grateful

About the Author

Andrea L. Dudley
Author, Speaker, Transformation Coach

Whether it's a small change or a life transformation, Andrea finds so much joy in helping others discover their true place in this world. She considers herself a transformation coach and speaker, but really she's so much more. When it comes to new ideas and God-given purposes, she's an enthusiastic leader who inspires others to bring their visions to life. From personal dilemmas to relationship drama, Andrea is absolutely dedicated to coming alongside others and helping them find love and beauty in all things. Contentment. Radiance. Joy. That's what she wants for everyone.

Her undeniable passion for people and her holistic-faith based approach embodies a bold message of empowerment, inspiration, and spirituality that is a catalyst for success and accomplishment. As the CEO of Habakkuk Publishing, Andrea has also helped over 130 people became newly published authors and her signature writing and publishing program, Birth Your Book In 90 days, effectively (and simply!) teaches authors how to self-publish their work.

A dynamic and creative speaker, you can find Andrea featured in the BEST Conference, SOAR women's conference, and W.I.L conference. She has an acute sense of empathy and a level of spiritual sensitivity that can zero in on the unique needs of her audience and meet them where they are. Because of this, women always leave changed. Inspired. Ready for their destinies.

She is also a profound leader with vast network marketing skills and a beautiful singer. Her voice has literally taken her around the world as she's performed everywhere from South Africa to Greece and so many places between.

No matter where she goes or what she's doing, however, the heart of her message stays with her. Andrea firmly believes that we need to invest in another person's vision to truly succeed. This is why she joined the volunteer staff for the Radical Success Institute with Steve Harvey and Doreen Rainey and commits herself to always giving back and helping others live their dreams. When it comes down to it, Andrea is a lover of life and people. Merging those two things together, she is a passionate speaker and transformation coach who fully devotes herself to everyone who crosses her path. Because it's in helping others shine that we find our own true strength and beauty as well.

Over the years I have received words of prophecy and most have been "right on". This one, from Apostle Jane Hamon, is probably the most thorough and accurate that I have received to date.

For me, prophecy is very personal and intimate and something that I don't usually share but I was prompted by the Holy Spirit to open up my heart and my life to you so that you can know me more personally.

"And it shall come to pass in the last days, God declares, that I will pour out of My Spirit upon all mankind, and your sons and your daughters shall prophesy [telling forth the divine counsels] and your young men shall see visions (divinely granted appearances), and your old men shall dream [divinely suggested] dreams", Acts 2:17 (Amplified Bible)

The prophecy...

"You are an anointed woman with an Elisha anointing to confront death with a double portion anointing and the Spirit of the Lord says daughter, You have confronted many things in your own life and your family's lives. You have watched the enemy come in and take some out before their time. I have put a God ordained divine hatred for the operation of the spirit of death inside of you. Daughter you will break the ways that death manifest as it begins to come and talk physical life and physical vitality. You will have a Miracle Ministry as I flow out of you, says the Spirit of God, through

your hands with a healing anointing. You will break death as it manifests through poverty. I will give you supernatural keys for prosperity not just for individuals, homes and families but for entire communities says the Spirit of God.

You will break the works of poverty and the works of death and destruction that try to drag families down into addictive patterns. Daughter I am going to cause you to be a Bold Lioness of the Lord to track down the enemy and break his power territorially. I have given you the capacity. Do not fear death. There was a time when you felt that spirit of death all around...you smelled it, you saw it, you sensed it. That is not today; this is a new season, this is a new day. As I have delivered you from death so you will deliver many others. At times you will cast spirits out, other times you will counsel and bring life and principles. There is a breaker anointing inside of you to break men and women free, to break children free and young ones free.

Daughter, Do not underestimate the power of my Spirit working in you and through you.

For you hate evil. I have put a divine hatred for evil in you.

As much as you love me and are passionate about me you will be passionate about destroying the works of the enemy. For this purpose the Son of Man was manifest that he might destroy the works of the devil.

Your heart is clicking in to the Love of God and the hatred of evil and you will see Mighty deliverance come through your hands.

Entire families and family lines will be delivered because of the passion I have put in you to see death defeated.

You will be even like Jesus that stood at the grave of Lazarus and said Lazarus come forth. The day will come when you will even raise the dead.

Those that have physically died you will call them back from the other side of the grave.

For I have put my Resurrection Life and my Resurrection Power in you."

Apostle Jane Hamon
Bethesda Bible Church
Women's Conference

CPSIA information can be obtained
at www.ICGtesting.com
Printed in the USA
FFOW02n2238180216
21625FF